At Home
on a Horse
in the Woods

A Journey into Living
Your Ultimate Dream

By
JANET WOLANIN ALEXANDER

TABLE OF CONTENTS

PART I: LATE ADULTHOOD

PART II: EARLY ADULTHOOD

PART III: CHILDHOOD

PART IV: LAST WORDS

APPENDICES

INTRODUCTION

Your Dream

Were you born with a mysterious dream that no one you knew shared or related to? Did you ever feel stuck and in need of an encouraging example?

Did all your struggles fail until, discouraged, you were tempted to give up your dream forever? I was on the verge—until a minister shared a crucial piece of wisdom with me. As soon as I accepted it, my dream began to manifest in the most unimagined way. That was 20 years ago, and I'm still living it!

If you can't seem to achieve your dream on your own, read on. Discover what the minister said to me. Apply it. And enjoy the manifestation of *your* dream.

My Dream

At Home on a Horse in the Woods traces my path to realizing my dream—horses. Each tale tells of an experience that touched my soul and demanded to be written—and shared. Some readers like to read a tale a day, whereas others prefer to read them all in one sitting.

My horse experiences may surprise you, for neither was I born into horses nor have I ever lived in the country. I've always been a boarder. I own neither a truck nor a horse trailer and ride the same trails over and over. My husband is not a horse person. And, after dabbling in dressage and endurance, I do not compete. My calling has been to develop and enjoy a deep relationship with a few horses.

My tales vary from serious to funny, from descriptions of nature to inner reflections, from realistic to fanciful, from happy to sad, from high to low, and from earthly to spiritual. They are all true, but names and places have been generalized resulting in "word paintings" more akin to watercolors than photography, hopefully allowing you to imagine yourself having a similar experience in your own locale.

If I had to conclude what my dream taught me, it would be that, as lovely as they are, horses are more than blood and bone: they are spirit guides who allow us to glimpse God and experience some of heaven on earth.

THE TALE BEHIND THE TALES

Although I've always felt compelled to write up my stand-out horse experiences, it wasn't until I retired and joined a writing group that I was inspired to compile them into a book. Was the purpose to preserve my memories in case of dementia in old age? To leave behind a legacy? To express gratitude to God? Finally, a fourth possibility popped up—maybe this book is supposed to serve others.

This realization was both exciting and terrifying because it meant that I would have to share my story with, gasp, strangers. Ultimately, I chose to do so in the faith that it will somehow, somewhere, speak to the kindred spirits who need to hear it, and we will no longer feel alone.

*Every decision I make is a choice between a
grievance and a miracle.
I let go of grievances and choose miracles.*

*(Deepak Chopra, The Spontaneous Fulfillment
of Desire, 2003, p.214.)*

DEDICATION

To all dreamers, may your visions manifest. And to the horse-crazy kids—young and old among you—may hoof beats finally accompany your heartbeats.

ACKNOWLEDGEMENTS

To my mother, who encouraged me to read; and my father, who encouraged me to write.

To my husband Jim for "getting" me and for bringing animals into my life.

To those mentioned and to those not who accompanied me on parts of my horse journey.

To colleagues (Frances, Ed, Phyllis, and Bev) who served as encouragers and editors while I was teaching.

To the Southern Indiana Writers, an eclectic group of wonderfully wrought characters with grand imaginations, who took over their role when I retired.

To Geronimo, Dancer's Streak, and Highlander—oh, the places you have taken me!

To the Unity Church for its teaching of positive, practical Christianity.

To both my publishers, Per Bastet (2017) and AAE (2019).

To the writer of my foreword, my endorsers, and my readers.

And to God, for knocking on my heart to let horses in.

AUTHOR ENDORSEMENTS

This gentle, introspective book explores the very special bond that occurs between humans and horses, as seen through the eyes of the author. She shares her own story with humor, empathy, and humility, giving readers a good look into the rather unique world of the horse-obsessed, from childhood pony to life-long companion. If you are a horse lover yourself, you will find this work especially enjoyable. If you're not, you will gain a much greater understanding of what motivates us to seek the company of these noble, incredibly powerful-yet-sensitive creatures and how we thrive, grow, and blossom as a result.

C.S. Marks, PhD, Professor Emerita, Equine Science, Author of The Elf Hunter Trilogy and The Alterra Histories.

With the drum of hoofbeats as a backdrop, it's a privilege and honor to experience life and the trail through Janet's love of horses and her memoir *At Home on a Horse in the Woods*. Thank you, Janet, for giving us all the courage to never quit believing in the power of faith and the childhood dream.

Amber Massey, Author of For the Love of Horses.

An inspiring memoir by a woman born with the dream of connecting with horses. Her determination and faith finally came to fruition—she met and shared adventures with three equine partners. *At Home on a Horse in the Woods* is a testament to the decision never to give up on your dream, no matter your age. Many women who think they are too old for life with a horse will be especially encouraged by this book. Remember, most dreams do come true when the time is right. And wishes can be horses!

Trudy Andrews, Author of the Aynslie McCallum Adventure Series One on the Island and Pony Tails and Other Short Stories.

FOREWORD

I'm not a horse person. If I *were* a horse person, there would be nothing wonderful in my loving this book. And I do love this book.

I love the connection Janet Alexander always felt with horses, even before she had come into personal contact with one. That speaks to the pull we all feel toward our souls' completion or our spiritual path or whatever you choose to call that activity, place, person, or entity that makes us feel whole.

I love the balance of humor and passion Alexander brings to each story. I love the way everything—be it butterflies, a moonlit ride, being utterly and literally befogged, or a packing peanut soaked in doe urine—has a deeper meaning and a fuller significance.

I love the people Alexander knows and has known, human people or equine people, who enrich her life and, through her stories, my life.

It was a joy to hear these pieces as she labored to word and punctuate them exactly right so their clarity could shine through. It's a joy to see them in print and to think of them bringing the same delight to other readers that they've brought to me.

Read.

Enjoy.

Marian Allen, author of The Wolves of
Port Novo and the Sage trilogy.

PART I

LATE ADULTHOOD

CHAPTER 1
MELTDOWN AND EPIPHANY

Hi. My name is Janet, and I'm addicted to horses. Always have been, and I suspect I always will be. Where my love for the critters came from is a mystery. I was born in a big northern city totally unconnected to horses and anyone even remotely associated with them—until one day, out of the blue, a year or two after my marriage at 43, enrolled in a class at my husband's church to learn more about his faith, I received the assignment to schedule a private meeting with a minister.

I was sitting in Reverend Judy's office when she invited me to talk about anything I wanted. What popped up was something I'd thought I successfully suppressed but which had recently raised its ugly head. I hesitated to share it with a person of the cloth—even one who had played an important part in my mixed-religious wedding. At best, she would find it silly or trivial, the world being so full of people with serious, life-and-death problems. At worst, if it's true that the earthly domain is merely a testing ground for eternal life in Heaven and the price of that prize is suffering and self-denial, she might even find it blasphemous. Despite my reluctance and feeling safe in Judy's presence, I quietly and tentatively began to speak.

During my warm up, I clued her in about my horse-crazy birth into a horseless environment: obtaining my youthful fixes by reading books, watching television Westerns, collecting statues, pasting newspaper and magazine pictures into scrapbooks, and how occasional experiences with flesh and blood horses had fanned my love into a passion.

I shared how I'd gone off to college and graduated at 21 with a teaching degree, debt free and with the family car—thanks to my generous, hardworking parents. I lived in a boarding house during my first year of teaching so I could buy my first horse. Then I sold him five years later to move out of state for grad school. The goal was to transition into a better-paying profession that would allow me deeper entry into the horse world.

After earning my master's degree, I found myself right back in teaching—this time with a student loan to pay back. And, despite the school's location among Louisville horse farms and its large rural campus where I enjoyed sharing my love of nature with my students, I had few opportunities to ride, let alone buy another horse, thus demonstrating the definition of insanity—repeating the same behavior and expecting a different result.

At this point in my monologue to Reverend Judy, I started picking up steam. It was torture driving past the farms to and from my apartment in the city. So was watching parents, dressed in equestrian garb and pulling horse trailers, drop off their kids before going riding. I confessed that I was jealous of the ones who'd been born into horses.

Reverend Judy was still calm and quiet, so I cut to the last straw. Not too long ago, a colleague looking for a good home for her well-trained, aging gelding, had offered him to me for a reasonable price. I rode and liked him, but, as much as I wanted another horse, the timing still wasn't right. My husband, like me, was a middle-aged, workaholic educator, whose job wasn't permanent, and we'd just recently taken on a mortgage. Both animal lovers, we knew the responsibility that came with animal ownership and that we were not in the position to take on a horse.

The experience still burned. *What kind of God would offer me such a wonderful opportunity, knowing I would have to turn it down? A very sick and cruel one, that's who!* My supposedly well-suppressed emotions churned and surfaced in rapid succession. I began to rant. My rant turned into a tirade. I talked faster and louder. *I'd absolutely HAD IT with God. I was SICK of being tormented by a sicko-psycho who enjoyed teasing me with tidbits only to snatch them away as soon as I reached for them. Jerking not one but two horses away was beyond cruel. Time was running short as I was now—gasp—middle-aged! Was it so wrong to want some more horse happiness during my waning years on this planet?*

Then and there, right in front of Revered Judy, I put God on notice. I informed the big bully that *I was no longer going to play the enabling victim in this game because I no longer wanted a horse. Horses were too frivolous, too expensive, too dangerous, and I was too old. So there,* I told God, *You can't hurt me any longer,* then reiterated, in case God hadn't caught on the first time, *I NO LONGER WANT A HORSE!*

My offering wasn't at all pretty, and it hadn't come easily, but I'd finally submitted my will to what I thought was God's, sacrificing my desire for horses and accepting my martyrdom. Truth be told, I was exhausted by trying and failing to bring horses into my life through my own efforts and had simply cried "uncle" and given up.

Emotionally spent, out of words, horrified and embarrassed at my irreverent, childish outburst, I looked at Reverend Judy and prepared for rebuke.

Unbelievably, Reverend Judy's demeanor hadn't changed—except for the addition of the gentle smile on her face! She leaned toward me and said these words, words I never would have predicted from a person in her profession, words spoken in a quiet, warm, loving voice: *"Jan, where do you think your love of horses comes from?"* After a short pause for me to consider the answer, she continued, *"God created it in you, and God will never stop knocking at your heart until you let horses in!"*

The room swirled, and the floor fell away. I couldn't speak. I was too numb to take in the lovely jolt of this mind-blower all at once. It had never occurred to me that the purpose of our earthly existence was to be happy so we can better express the uncountable facets of God here on Earth—itself perhaps a heaven, depending upon our thoughts, beliefs, and actions and their consequences! Could all this possibly be true? Now that my meltdown had burned the debris blocking my channel to God, it actually seemed plausible!

I slowly collected myself and drove back to the cozy, suburban house that Jim and I had just purchased from a friend, despite my reservation about moving to Southern Indiana. It was well built and cared for, and our mortgage payments were affordable, but it was still a financial commitment. Jim was home, and I told him right away what had happened. Despite not being a horse person, his immediate response was another surprise: "*We moved here because of the lower housing prices, so perhaps a horse and its upkeep are within budget. Research the costs, and we'll see if we can afford them.*"

God bless the man!

I called Amy, a horse acquaintance who lived near school. She told me to call Connie, who'd just moved to Indiana. As soon as I mentioned I was thinking of buying a horse, Connie told me that she and her husband were so busy training young horses that they could use someone to exercise their semi-retired champion on the trails of nearby state property! In a few moments, what had seemed impossible became possible—and in ways I never had imagined. Horses started flowing into my life and haven't stopped yet.

Late spring, 1999

CHAPTER 2
MY NEW MOUNT

Our love affair began on June 10, 1999. I was 47 and in mid-life crisis; he was a white-haired gentleman, semi-retired from a distinguished career. Who was the mystery man who stole his way into my heart that day and continues to further endear himself? He is none other than Dancer's Streak, a registered Arabian with the most beautiful equine name I have ever heard. I had absolutely no idea at the time how large an impact this small gelding was going to have on my life.

Horseless since my 20's and acutely aware of the accelerating advance of time, I knew that I had to act if I were ever going to reconnect with horses. A local horsewoman (Amy) introduced me to Dancer's owners, Connie and Mike, who invited me to ride with them. After our ride in a state forest, I was amazed to discover that Dancer was 21 years old. My journal entry for the day states that our first ride lasted two hours and *was a blast— fast-paced with lots of jumping over logs across the trail and that Dancer was a well-trained horse with lots of impulsion.*

I couldn't believe my good fortune when I was invited to ride him whenever I wanted. His owners were competitive endurance riders so involved with training their young horses that they needed someone to exercise Dancer. My awe of him grew when I learned that he was a 5,000-mile endurance champion, who had entered 100 endurance rides, including 13 one-day 100-milers. Even more astounding, he had completed 91 of the rides and finished in the top ten 71 times, earning 18 Firsts and eight Best Conditions! In 1989, he earned a perfect score of 100 points on his first and only competitive trail ride, set the record for the five-day, 250-mile Michigan Shore to Shore Endurance Ride (22 hours and seven minutes), and was named the Southwest Regional Endurance Champion!

Too bad that Dancer hadn't been born with a built-in odometer— I wonder how many miles of conditioning he had racked up in addition to those 5,250 miles. How awesome to become responsible for keeping such a phenomenal horse in shape during retirement.

Dancer and Me, 2001

Tale excerpted from my nomination for the American Endurance Ride Conference's 2003 Equine Hall of Fame Award. (Dancer's Streak was not selected.)

CHAPTER 3
FALL EVENING MAGIC

In Fall, 2000, I took a course at my husband's church offered by Reverend Carole. When she announced that the last class would be a talent show, I panicked—I wasn't a singer, dancer, painter, sculptor, tailor, knitter, magician, crotchetier, comedian, acrobat, musician, or anything out of the ordinary—and had no talents to share! After taking a deep breath, I decided to apply what I was learning about practical Christianity: thinking positively, not negatively; being grateful for what I had, instead of focusing on things I felt I lacked; and living in the now, instead of the past or the future. I asked myself what I most loved to do with the intention of sharing it. Two things came to mind—riding and writing—so I tried to take my non-equestrian classmates on a vicarious fall trail ride.

It is late afternoon on a dry, hot day at the end of October. You have just arrived at your friends' farm after a long day of work, errands, and rush-hour traffic. You quickly grab a halter and lead rope from the barn and hurry to the pasture. Your mount, Dancer's Streak, doesn't run away from you but neither does he walk toward you. When you reach him, you quickly slip his halter over his head and walk him to the barn. You thread his lead rope through a metal ring on the outside wall and tie a slipknot.

With a flattened hand, you offer Dancer a carrot. The tensions of the day melt away as you comb his thin, yellowing mane and brush his white coat, just beginning to thicken for the winter.

9

Your pulse and your breathing slow. You check his hooves for packed debris, such as stones, then swing your saddle onto his back, and fasten the girth. You switch Dancer's halter to his bridle and lead him back into the pasture. After retightening his girth, you mount. As you slowly ride to the back of the rear pasture, you admire the expanses of verdant grass and azure sky.

Dancer passes through the grass so quietly that two deer are startled. In a flash, they flick their white tails and bound away. Presently, you come to a gate leading into the woods. You consciously divest yourself of any remaining worries or concerns—the gate is too narrow to accommodate your baggage, and you certainly don't want to impose it on your mount. A horse named Dancer deserves a rider who, like him, is light, relaxed, and present in the moment. Once in the forest, you inhale a deep breath of pure air. The light is dimmer in the woods, and the temperature is refreshingly cooler. The autumn leaves delight you. Those still on the trees are sunlit shades of yellow and gold. Those that have fallen crunch loudly as Dancer rustles through them. Although the sound obscures the rhythmic touchdown of Dancer's hooves, the cadence rocks your hips and lower back. Here, among the trees, you feel at home—peaceful, happy, and at ease.

You prompt Dancer into a slow, warm-up trot. He pauses at the base of the hill and needs a little encouragement to cross the creek. Then it's a straight shot across the meadow and through the woods to a road. You turn right onto the blacktop and distinctly hear the gentle clip-clop of hooves whose shoes have recently been pulled. Shortly, after a curve in the road, you make a left turn back into the forest and begin a working trot, then a canter, up a gradual hill. A couple of fallen logs lie across the trail and you laugh as Dancer energetically jumps them.

At the half-way point, you stop and listen before reversing direction. Two crows are cawing. The crickets are chirping more loudly. The sun is setting along the ridge. Dancer was born with an internal compass—no matter how lost you get on the trails, he always knows the most direct way home. He now wants to get there quickly and, because he hasn't been ridden in a week, that's at a full gallop. You let him—and yourself—go. You feel gloriously young and free. In a flash, you're back at the road. Once you reenter the forest, Dancer really surprises you. In another burst of speed, he gallops even faster—almost to the gate. His energy is contagious. You slow to a safe walk and reenter the back pasture. It feels so open compared to the dense forest. And it's still light here, although the once all-blue sky is now streaked with salmon, peach, and violet, and a thin crescent moon has replaced the sun. Somehow, over the screaming of a killdeer, the horses in the front pasture sense Dancer's return and whinny. You continue riding slowly to cool him down. Dancer stops for a moment to bite an itch on a front leg. When he raises his head; he exhales audibly in a series of lip-sputtering snorts.

A few horses in the front pasture follow as you head toward the barn. You dismount and *shoosh* them away so you can lead Dancer out of the gate. Outside the barn, you replace his halter and retie him. You remove his saddle and recheck his hooves. Then you feed him an apple to reward him for a great ride. You are astonished at the potency of the smell released when Dancer bites the McIntosh in half. You wipe some of the sweat off his back, neck, and chest with a damp sponge and then towel him dry. You lead him into his pasture and remove his halter. True to form, he carefully chooses a spot, and, after circling it several times, ever so slowly kneels, then rolls, first onto his side, then his back. He pleasurably celebrates the relief from your weight by rubbing his head and body against the dry earth. Then he rises and shakes vigorously. Oh well, at least he was clean for the past hour!

All the horses line up at the feed buckets spaced out along the fence's inner side. You pour grain into each and enjoy hearing the shadowy apparitions munch down their starlit dinner. Up above, you recognize the Big Dipper, Cassiopeia's jagged 'M' (or 'W' or a Greek sigma), and Cepheus's childlike house. You know that Pegasus is up there somewhere too, and, once home, resolve to ask your amateur-astrologer husband to point out the sky horse to you. Nightfall is a sacred time of day. Totally calm and relaxed, you are grateful to the Creator for a magical evening.

October, 2000. Original version published in The Trail Rider, November/December, 2002

CHAPTER 4
SPRING AFTERNOON REVERIE

I enjoyed writing my first horse tale and hearing my classmates' reactions, so I complied when Spirit prompted me to write more. From 2002-2006, nine of my tales were published in horse magazines. Although I received no payment, I was encouraged by their acceptance and seeing my name in print.

Many of my students and fellow teachers went to Florida and the Caribbean for their spring break. Me? I enjoyed my spring fling in the hills of Southern Indiana.

April 11th started on a good note and built to a mid-afternoon crescendo. In the morning, I test drove a bicycle, for sale by a fellow bike-club member. His carbon composite road bike was smaller and lighter than my aluminum-steel hybrid. Flying up and down hills on a 25-mile bike ride was a good warm-up for my afternoon itinerary—riding Dancer.

But, instead, a surprise awaited me. Dancer's owners asked me to ride Smoke, a light gray gelding with a charcoal mane and tail. I'd only ridden the Anglo-Arab once before—on a training ride with them. But because he'd made such a good impression and has such a great reputation, I readily agreed. I was thrilled at being entrusted to take him out on my own.

Smoke stood calmly at the hitching post—until I bent to move the garden hose he was standing on. After a little panic dance at the slithering green "snake," Smoke let me groom and saddle him. He didn't move as I mounted, a definite etiquette plus. Smoke was so much taller than Dancer that it was a stretch for me, a six-footer, to lift my left leg up to the stirrup.

"So far, so good," I thought. Then, in the back pasture, I faced my first (and only) problem—how to get Smoke to sustain a trot, the preferred gait of many endurance riders. He kept popping into a slow, smooth canter, a less efficient gait that expends more energy in hilly terrain. Once he maintained the preferred gait, we entered the forest and descended a long hill. There, a toad hopping across the trail cast a spell upon us. We slowed to a walk and began pleasure riding. My attention was drawn to the forest floor, where I recognized friends I hadn't seen since last spring. First were stands of May-apples, their leaf whorls resembling parasols in various stages of extension. Then came splotches of bluets. I love the simplicity and color of these Quaker-ladies—a tiny, cornflower-blue X with a pale, yellow center. Next were toad shade trilliums, each sporting three burgundy petals and three green leaves. Yellow violets and white cut-leaf toothworts were scattered about. A purple violet adjacent to a bluet struck me as an interesting color combination but not one I would have put together.

My eyes rose to the understory trees. The fuchsia redbud blossoms were in their prime and the creamy dogwood flowers just beginning to open. A mysterious tree, popcorned with small white flowers, caught my attention. I longed to know its name (and looked it up later—serviceberry). I could only see the sky partially through the trees, which were just beginning to leaf out. Once the leaves grew to full size, little sunlight would penetrate to the forest floor. The parade of wildflowers hadn't much time to complete its march. I felt fortunate to catch spring in mid-step.

Each year at this time, I consider assigning leaf collections to my students. Why do I always wait until fall when the leaves are wind-torn and bug-eaten, many too large to fit onto a standard-sized sheet of paper? Why not preserve specimens in their tiny, fragile, fresh perfection?

As I projected my vision across to the surrounding hills, it was obvious that the terrain was in mid shift from the empty browns and grays of winter to the overwhelming profusion of dark summer green. The hillsides were priming in green pastels.

Time slowed to the rhythm of Smoke's hoofbeats and my breathing. I was fully living in the present, not evaluating the past nor planning the future. I was very calm. Occasionally, I felt the splat of a raindrop. The wind assaulted us on the ridges. The still, humid air partially smothered us in the valleys.

I continued to spot wildflowers. I easily recalled the names of some species, such as Dutchman's-breeches, their pantaloon blossoms hanging upside down to dry. Others were old acquaintances I'd met before whose names I could narrow down but not recall with certainty—the buttercup-like flowers on the stream bank and either a celandine poppy or a marsh marigold. When Smoke and I circled back to the toad crossing, I marveled at a fiddlehead of a fern delicately uncurling. I searched my brain for the name of the mustard lighting up the field (winter cress). Then another unusual color combination struck me—fresh redbud flowers backed by last fall's liver-colored sumac berries. Not yet ready to break the toad's spell, Smoke and I added a loop to our return trip to the barn. Back in the woods, I noticed clumps of spring beauties, their white petals striped like peppermints, and yellow trout lilies, named for their mottled leaves.

I was immensely grateful for the luxury of an entire day outdoors enjoying spring. What a coincidence it was to ride two new mounts on the same day. Which did I prefer? The horse, of course! As much fun as it is to ride a bike on a road, it's pure bliss to explore wooded trails on the back of an equine. I, for one, bond better with flesh than metal!

April, 2001. Original version published in The Trail Rider, May/ June, 2002

CHAPTER 5
HIGHLANDER

Through Dancer's owner, Connie, I met Lois, another competitive long-distance rider with a string of horses at different levels of training. In early 2000, I got to ride her semi-retired competitive trail champion as well as Highlander, an "accident" produced when a young Walker stallion got into an Arabian mare's pasture.

In October, I rode the now-5½-year-old gelding in a 25-mile (limited distance) endurance ride. I cherish this photo of us trotting down a dusty forest trail on a picture-perfect fall day.

My husband had an enlargement of "On Cloud Nine" framed for my birthday. I love the rainbow assortment of tack I borrowed to outfit him!

Fall, 2000

Highlander and Me, 2000
Becky Pearman Photography

CHAPTER 6
SUMMER NIGHT ENCHANTMENT

It was dark out, and the two of us women were miles away from our vehicle. Were we scared? Heck, no! Both teachers, we were too busy enjoying our last Monday night get-together of summer vacation. Besides, we were in good company—Galant Legacy (AKA Legs), Highlander, and Nova were with us. Legs and Highlander are endurance horses; Nova is a herding dog, a blue heeler, to be exact. To beat the oppressive heat and humidity, the five of us had left the campground parking lot around 7:15 for a 16-mile training ride in the woods. An hour and a half later, we were trotting toward a huge orange sun teetering atop a hill. Soon afterward, it got dark. Because the waning moon wouldn't rise for several hours, we slowed down and began relying on our night vision to navigate.

My riding companion was Lois, a phenomenal woman. In addition to being a teacher, she is a wife, mother, grandmother, committed member of her church, and a horsewoman extraordinaire. Next to each other, we look like Mutt and Jeff. She's just under five feet tall, while I am a tad over six. Lois may be tiny in stature and quiet in personality, but she is one tough rider. The little dynamo lives to win 50 and 100-mile endurance races. I, on the other hand, have only ridden in two 50-milers and just for completion. Her horses, both chestnut geldings with white blazes, parallel us in height. Legs is a petite, 14.3 hand, full-blooded Arabian, while Highlander is a sturdy, 15.2, half Arab-half Tennessee Walker.

The forest took on a whole new personality in the dark. The swarms of stalking horseflies disappeared. (Most riders crunch the flies against their horses and let the dead carcasses drop to the ground. Me? I incapacitate mine as delicately as possible and zip them into my fanny pack for future science lessons!) The peaceful sound of chirping crickets replaced the irritating whine of blood-thirsty flies. The temperature cooled, the humidity lowered, and the colors faded. At first, we could see well enough to trot slowly over the saplings that had fallen across the trail. Then, for safety, we slowed to a walk. We automatically silenced our voices as if we had entered a dim cathedral where speaking was irreverent.

Hearing kicked in to supplement our dwindling sight. Gravel was gray and crunchy; packed dirt, tan and quiet; mud, dark and squishy. We recognized streams by the firefly larvae glowing along the shore and the reflection of tree tops in the water. Occasionally, flying adults signaled just ahead of us and heat lightning flashed in the distance. We neither saw nor heard any signs of civilization.

I had lost track of Nova. Lois and Legs began fading in and out of view in front of me. Sometimes they looked like dark, dense, floating masses. But, every now and again, the moon revealed glimpses of Legs' white saddle pad, crupper, and left hind sock, or it reflected off Lois's bare arms. When Lois and Legs disappeared altogether, I was never fearful or anxious; I simply trusted that they were still there. (I know there's a lesson in this, but I'm not clear what it is. To trust in my unknown future? To "let go" more often? To have faith? If so, in what? I already believe in God.)

My sphere of concentration shrank to my immediate area. Instead of chasing off trail, Nova now stayed glued to Highlander. I fixated upon the white star on his forehead. It was the only part of him that I could see—his silver-gray body had disappeared.

I shifted all my attention to my sense of feel. I became so physically comfortable that I lost total awareness of my body. Highlander's steady cadence had rocked me into a meditative state. I felt at peace, safe in the blackness of Mother Nature's womb. What bliss this unanticipated moment was!

The spell broke as we neared the highway and started hearing traffic. Soft music and a flickering campfire greeted us when we returned to the parking lot at around 10:00. Reluctantly, we halted in the middle of the grassy clearing. While the horses grazed, we, still mounted, gazed at the stars that filled the sky.

I felt disoriented when I dismounted and quickly shifted my focus back to the distant sky. So many more stars were visible here than at my suburban home! I panicked at only recognizing one constellation and not recalling its name (Cassiopeia). It wasn't until the horses were in the trailer and we were en route to the barn, my head hanging unsafely out of the truck's passenger window, that I found the Big Dipper and relaxed, assured that the universe was still in its proper order.

August, 2001. Original version published in The Trail Rider, September/October, 2002

CHAPTER 7
FLIGHTS OF WINTER FANCY

My eyes had to be deceiving me! Surely the scene before us was a mirage, most likely introduced by the unseasonably warm weather! The wooded ridge trail upon which Sue, Lois, and I had been riding our horses couldn't have transported us across the ocean! Yet, the image of an alpine storybook village remained when we dismounted to survey it from a more grounded perspective. I felt like Hansel and Gretel stumbling unexpectedly upon a homestead in the middle of a European forest. Mesmerized, what else could my friends and I do but tie Hoosier, Galant Legacy, and Highlander to the gate at the end of the trail and step into the clearing? We couldn't resist exploring. Instead of candy and gingerbread, the chalet-style buildings were sturdily constructed from planks of stained wood. Each had a steeply pitched roof lined with small, curling wooden shingles housing colonies of lichen. Immediately in front of the gate was a small cottage flanked by an outhouse with the signature crescent moon carved out of the door. A sidewalk with a metal railing zigzagged partially down the slope east of the buildings. It ended at a quaint chapel with leaded glass windows patterned with large dogwood blossoms. Uphill from the outhouse was a bunkhouse. At the very top of the path rose a large, multi-story lodge. A walk to the front of the building revealed that the lodge stood upon a precipitous rock outcropping on the edge of a hill that plunged into a vast valley to the south and west. The unexpected and majestic view was breathtaking. We were enjoying it from the lower of two large decks. The ground beneath us was thickly littered with skeet shells.

While I was in fairyland, Lois was reliving her past. Unlike me, she had grown up in this area and was remembering the foxhunters' lodge that existed here when she was a child. Then she was recalling memories of the current lodge when her cousin owned it during the 1980s. She was singing hymns in the chapel with members of her church and eating meals with her extended family in the lodge. She was seated at a massive table under a giant chandelier in front of a large fireplace; her children were playing with their cousins on the hardwood floor.

Sue? She was engrossed in reading the names and dates carved into the rock face between the two decks.

The setting sun signaled that it was time for us to go. It would soon be dark, and the trailhead where the horse trailer was parked was eight miles away. As soon as we completed our circle around the lodge and the horses were back in view, my mind leaped from Europe to a town in America's Old West, and I was swaggering down a packed-dirt Main Street toward the mount I had left tied to a hitching post.

Thus far, our adventure had mainly taken place in black and white. The trunks and bare limbs of the deciduous trees, as well as the buildings now behind us, were various shades of ash. The trails were gravel-gray or dirt-brown, the leaf litter on the forest floor was dull russet. These muted colors had been broken only occasionally by dark green pine needles, fluorescent green patches of moss, and the pale yellow sun.

The sunset was now giving us a more dramatic reprieve from the monotony, a show before the blackness of night. The orange sun nestled in the valley between two ridges far off to our left. It was enveloped in a long, watermelon-pink cloud topped by a beautiful fuchsia one. Our cheers of admiration broke the silence of the winter woods.

We rode so fast along the ridge that I morphed into a celestial being riding Pegasus through the sky. It was dark when the horses and accompanying dogs slowed to descend the switchback into the valley below. I glanced up and saw a canine silhouette running along the ridge. Was it Lois's dog? Or had the constellation Canis Major dropped to earth and taken on flesh?

Once in the valley, we picked up a trot. A spark flew from one of Hoosier's shoes after striking a rock, and Highlander's hind hooves occasionally clicked when they forged against his front ones. By the time we returned to the trailer, the crescent moon missing from the outhouse was in the sky, along with a sprinkle of twinkling stars.

What an exhilarating evening reverie!

February, 2002. Original version published in The Trail Rider, January/February, 2003

CHAPTER 8
BARN SLEEPOVER HIGHLIGHTS

As time went by, I rode Dancer less and Highlander more. On my 50th birthday, Jim and I bought Highlander. Because we didn't have a horse trailer, we moved him to the new stable opening on a ridge across from a trailhead. Occasional long-distance rides (endurance and competitive trail) were headquartered next door. In April, 2002, I asked Wannettia and Marshall, owners of the stable, if I could sleep in their barn the weekend that Highlander and I planned to compete in back-to-back (Saturday and Sunday) 25-milers.

Friday Night, Just Him and Me: I laughed when I first saw my accommodations. My bedroom was the box stall where Highlander's grain and hay were stored on wooden pallets. Several bales, pushed crosswise against a wall and covered with a blanket, comprised my bed. Adjoining it was a TV tuned to the weather. Clamped above was a work light for reading and writing, and on a small table was a tablet of stationery! I laughed over and over after shutting myself in my stall for the night. Highlander, who remained free to patrol the open barn aisle and pasture at will, kept sticking his head in to check on me!

I fell asleep listening to country sounds: a chorus of chirping tree frogs, the "Who cooks for you, who cooks for you all?" questioning of a barred owl, and so many enthusiastic repetitions of another bird's reply, "Whip poor will! Whip poor will!" that I lost count.

I awoke around 4:00 a.m. to rain pelting on the metal roof. I found my shadow of a horse grazing in the dark pasture and shut him in his end stall for breakfast. Walking out of the barn, then going back into the barn, was like exiting and reentering a drum—the sound of the rain was much louder inside than out. It soon dissipated. After I crawled back into my sleeping bag, I was soothed to sleep by the lullaby of rain gently falling on grass. Just before dawn, I arose to the alarm of one very insistent rooster.

* * *

Saturday Night, Company: Two horses arrived after Saturday morning's 25-mile ride. First was Bud, a stranger from West Virginia. Stalling Bud, but not Highlander, did not work. Highlander stood outside Bud's door vigorously disapproving of the stranger's invasion of his private domain. Highlander, a pasture horse only used to confinement during feedings, had to be stalled for the night. But his stall was next to the one Bud was in, and that didn't work either; Bud had to be moved to a stall across the aisle.

Peace prevailed when Sue came and put her horse, Sparky, into the vacated stall next to Highlander's. All night long, the two buddies, with their heads huddled together in the aisle, plotted who-knows-what conspiracies.

I retired to a whippoorwill, fixating again on its name, and the distant booming of "Thunder Over Louisville," a fireworks display announcing that lightning-fast horses would soon run the Derby. The rains returned about 1:00 am, and I was glad for my dry, sweet-smelling bed.

* * *

Sunday Afternoon, Parting Company: Highlander and Bud, who had bonded on the morning's 25-miler, were in their stalls resting when Bud's owner came to take him home. (Sparky was still out on the 50-mile course.) Highlander became distraught when Bud left. As soon as the pasture gate was safely shut behind Bud, I let Highlander out of his stall. He galloped toward Bud, whinnying pitifully. My horse, who had only 24 hours ago rebelled at the usurper's invasion, was now begging him to return!

* * *

After Sparky and I left, Highlander regained dominion of the stable, again relying for companionship solely upon its owners, who had had two more stalls in their new barn "christened" the night before.

April, 2002. Original version published in The Trail Rider, March/ April, 2003

CHAPTER 9
WINTER REFLECTIONS

*W*inter *is a wonderful time for slow pleasure rides. The uncertain footing demands that Highlander and I proceed slowly. This allows us to fully engage our senses and concentrate on taking in enough of the winter woods to sustain us through another round of cabin fever and pasture monotony.*

Because of the unpredictable weather, road conditions, and early sunsets, I only get to ride once a week during winter. It's not enough!

* * *

Stream Ice, January 12: The shallow stream crossings were iced over. Highlander, a good drinker I've nicknamed Fish, hesitated at first. He lowered his head—only to find ice instead of water. He licked the ice and then cautiously placed a front hoof upon it. The foot slipped forward. Highlander picked it up, set it back down, applied some weight, and crunched a hole into the ice. After sipping some water, he continued this step-punch-drink sequence all the way across the stream. Then, he turned around and repeated it back!

The widest stream wasn't completely iced over. A gorgeous mosaic of interlocking frost "fingers" lined both shores, reaching toward but not yet connecting with those opposite.

* * *

Puddle Ice, February 1: A long puddle in a tire rut cut into the trail was crusted over with ice. Highlander's nose easily broke through the thin crust at the beginning and plowed through all the way to the puddle's end!

I think Highlander prefers puddle water to stream water because it's warmer and muddier. Why he likes to grab quick bites of mud along the trail is a mystery to me—salt and mineral blocks are available at his stable.

* * *

Sunset in the Pines, February 8: Riding through the pine forest always feels holy to me—like we're riding through an empty cathedral. Today was a special treat because snow covered the ground, and patches of bright blue sky peeked through the lacy green canopy. I felt like a mere mite riding an ant across the surface of a vast white candle bursting with fat wicks. As Highlander walked forward, the flame of the midafternoon sun passed from the tip of one tree-wick to the next.

* * *

Downhill Skiing, February 13: The trails were covered by a thick layer of wet snow. At the crest of a long, steep hill, "something" told me to dismount. About a third of the way down, Highlander and I both lost traction. I slid, and he skied down the next third of the hill. Fortunately, we both managed to stay upright and come to a standstill at the same time. Later, along a level trail, Highlander went into bloodhound mode. He lowered his head and skimmed it just above the ground, not to track any of the animals that had recorded their passage in the snow, but to occasionally dip and grab a mouthful of flakes.

At the end of the ride, after I turned Highlander out, he rolled in the pasture's white powder, making an equine snow angel. He created a brief blizzard when he rose to his feet and shook himself.

* * *

The Colors of Winter, undated: I appreciate color the most during the winter when it's a luxury. The smallest swatch is a luscious visual feast. My next quilt will be an abstract reflection of nature. Each quarter will feature the palette of a particular season.

The winter quadrat will be done in ash (tree trunks), fluorescent green (moss), white (snow), forest green (pine needles), sage (lichen), and russet (pockets of deciduous leaf litter showing through the tattered spread of snow).

* * *

Quiet and Peace, undated: The soggy leaves have long lost their fall crunch. The guns of hunting season are still. No insects sound. The songbirds have migrated.

I love the peace and privacy of winter riding—Highlander and I are the only two creatures in existence and have the whole world to ourselves.

As much as I also love spring, it always comes as a bit of a shock—we have to share the woods with invaders, the fair-weather riders cropping up with the wildflowers!

* * *

Epilog: Despite my last sentence, let it be known that I love to ride with a friend or two as much as I love riding alone. I love to ride, period! One advantage of riding alone, however, is sharing quality time and further bonding with one's horse.

March, 2003. Original version published in The Trail Rider, May/ June, 2003

CHAPTER 10
A COSMIC JOKE

Today's trail conditions favored amphibians more than horses. The mud soup was pocked with deep hoof prints left behind by many previous passersby. The goo tried to suck Highlander's shoes off each time he pulled his hooves out of the fresh churnings. When Highlander stopped at a stream crossing to drink, I noticed a toad swimming toward us. It eventually changed course, perhaps cued, not by our shadow (it was overcast), but by the current Highlander was creating with his lapping tongue?

A bit farther down the trail and right in front of us, another toad—suddenly and obliviously—hopped onto the trail and began crossing. I couldn't stop Highlander from stepping on it with a front hoof. (What were the mathematical odds of that?) I jumped off him and slogged like a drunkard over to the toad's vanishing point. I bent down and thrust my right hand into the cold mud. No toad. I plunged my hand into surrounding hoof prints too. I pulled up wads of mud, but, alas, no little critter. Where was it? Had the toad survived being pressed into the mud by a 1200-pound mammal?

I tried to convince myself that the odds were in the amphibian's favor. After all, hadn't it just survived the winter buried deeply in mud, absorbing oxygen through its skin? Surely, the toad would quickly work its way up to the surface and resume breathing through its nostrils. Why, perhaps the toad had even found sanctuary on its journey back down into the mud—in the concave sole of Highlander's hoof, a place that contains a rubbery, shock-absorbing triangle of tissue.

I laughed when I got the joke—the triangle's anatomical name? The frog!

April, 2003

CHAPTER 11
C.S. LEWIS AND PLEASURE RIDING

Trail riding took on a whole new dimension the spring after I read *The Chronicles of Narnia,* by C.S. Lewis. The seven-book, pre-Harry-Potter series, written in England between 1939 and 1956, records the adventures of several British children in a world populated by talking animals and mythological creatures.

My favorite books in *The Chronicles* are *The Magician's Nephew* and *A Horse and His Boy,* because, of course, they feature horses. In the latter, which should be co-titled *A Mare and Her Girl,* two children flee a hostile country on talking Narnian horses. I smiled when the boy's horse gives him riding lessons; laughed when the boy, forced at one point to ride an ordinary horse, comes to fully appreciate his instructor and concurred with the pacing advice he was given during a long-distance ride.

My favorite passage in the series, however, occurs in the first and most well-known book, *The Lion, The Witch and The Wardrobe,* when Aslan, the lion-creator of Narnia, takes two girls on a ride. The resulting flight of fancy weaves equine and leonine imageries into pure whimsical delight.

How exactly was my riding affected? My imagination was activated! My horse, Highlander, and I morphed into a centaur exploring our magic kingdom, a forest in Southeastern Indiana.

The maples, oaks, hickories, and tulip poplars became giant broccoli stalks; the holes in their trunks were the homes of gnomes; spider webs, strung across the trails, were "no trespassing" barricades; the slicing, bloodsucking deer flies were military patrol squadrons enforcing the arachnids' warnings; the loud droning of cicadas was an orchestra of dentists drilling patients' teeth; a wood thrush's song transposed into the fluid notes of a flute; a scattering of mushrooms, with flat, bright-yellow tops, doubled as empty bar tables in a closed café; the blossoms of Queen Anne's lace in the adjoining field were their tattered tablecloths laid out to dry; the thistle flowers adjoining them, from which thirsty fritillary butterflies greedily guzzled nectar, were magenta goblets; a bird pecking on a hollow tree was an operator tapping out a telegram.

One day the following May, Highlander and I were innocently trotting down the trail when crazed caterpillars, suspended on silk strands from the overhead branches, tried to strangle us! As we passed, the gauntlet of invertebrate trapeze artists, lassoers, and bungee jumpers dropped onto us. They tried to knit our top and bottom eyelashes together and sew our nostrils and mouths shut. Biting larvae landed on my neck and tried to inch their way down my shirt. I frantically tried to claw them and their silk off before Highlander and I were mummified alive! What fun it's been to have my imagination stimulated into overdrive!

* * *

Epilog: In addition to being a writer, C.S. Lewis was a religious scholar and a convert from atheism to Christianity. *The Chronicles* have underlying religious symbolism—Narnia, for example, represents Heaven. Riding Highlander in the woods is Narnia to me!

May, 2003. Original version published in The Trail Rider, September/ October, 2003. Another version published in 2013 in Pair of Normal What?, the 18th volume of the Indian Creek Anthology Series of the Southern Indiana Writers.

CHAPTER 12
MY SPIRIT GUIDES

How do you picture angels? As the Renaissance painters did—winged humanoids flying between heaven and earth? Or like the TV show "Touched by an Angel"—doves morphing into human form? And from where do your angels come—the far reaches of a celestial heaven or from your intuition?

The notion of a winged horse appeared centuries ago in Greek and Roman mythology and is still popular today. Here in Louisville, the Pegasus Parade precedes the Kentucky Derby each spring.

To me, Pegasus connotes a strong companion capable of carrying me into the unknown, a normally mute teacher who speaks volumes when I remain quiet long enough to listen. The winged horse symbolizes the power of the thoughts I give flight to. They are powerful because they help create my reality. Positive, divinely-inspired thoughts elevate me above my limited state of being; negative, egotistical thoughts plunge me into difficulty.

Remember Icarus? His father, Daedalus, constructed wax-and-willow-stem wings for their escape from the island of Crete. He instructed Icarus to fly a steady middle course over the sea—not too close to the waves and not too close to the hot sun. Instead, Icarus chose an undulating course with steep climbs and dives, ultimately melting off his wings and losing his life.

I'd spent decades repeatedly pursuing and repressing my attraction to horses, and, just as I was about to give them up for good, met a religious leader who suggested they were my God-given calling. My drowning spirit soared, and a white horse danced into my life.

Dancer's Streak will always have a special place in my heart. The image of him as Pegasus was indelibly imprinted upon me one evening years ago as we sprinted up a hill. The setting sun was hovering just above the crest, its intense rays illuminating us like a fan of spotlights. Almost blinded, all I could see was white—that of the light and Dancer's head and neck. Not able to see the ground, I became spatially disoriented. Unbound by gravity, we were flying!

Horses are such great medicine. They make me feel young again. Watching them intrigues and amuses me. Touching them soothes and grounds me. Listening to them while they feed calms and relaxes me.

How awesome it is that such powerful creatures trust and want to please us and are so gentle with us. Riding one through the woods is liberating—the chief way I unwind and reduce stress. Trail riding is both a good physical workout and good therapy. It's also very meditative, perhaps because it's through nature that God mainly speaks to me, perhaps because riding my horse is about the only time I fully live in the present.

Where will horses next lead me? I hope to the fulfillment of some other dreams—owning property adjacent to public land with extensive horse trails, owning a truck and a trailer so I can ride in new places, building a home in the country, and writing a book in my home library as my horses peacefully graze outside the window.

Who or what are the angels in your life? And what thoughts do you give flight to?

2002

CHAPTER 13
MY WALKS TO EMMAUS

S hortly after Highlander's move to his new stable, he and I exclusively became trail riders. I had enjoyed the excitement and speed of long-distance training rides and competitions, learning new things and meeting good people, but looked forward to quiet rides, focusing on nature, as we more slowly passed through it.

The theme of a recent Sunday sermon was the walk to Emmaus. As the minister recounted the New Testament story about the two disciples encountering but not recognizing Jesus on the road after his resurrection, my mind returned to the retreat center I visited last July. One afternoon I was asked to choose a partner and accompany her on an Emmaus Walk through the center's lovely campus. During our hour together, we took turns non-verbally leading and following each other, the entire time treating each other as Jesus.

This reverie was interrupted by a startling goose-bump revelation: Last summer's Emmaus Walk wasn't my first and only one—I've been going on Emmaus Walks for years! Why, every time Highlander and I traverse the trails of the forest, we're on an Emmaus Walk (Trot, Canter, or Gallop). In close physical contact and companionable silence, he and I enjoy life and appreciate the beauty of God's creation together. Riding is a form of prayer!

2003. Original version published in Trail Blazer, November 15, 2003.

Chapter 14

ILLUMINATION

Highlander and I fell into a weeknight riding routine when school started in August. Morning rides were no longer possible; night riding was the only way to avoid the late afternoon heat and the annoying horse flies. Another advantage was that trails approaching monotony by day became almost new at night but retained a comforting sense of familiarity.

The spiritual dimension of our new routine became apparent on the very first ride. The evening was cloudy and humid. Rain was definitely on its way, and I gambled on getting back before it hit. Highlander and I left at dusk, trotting fast to make time while light remained. We were deep into the woods when it got dark. Unexpectedly, a flash of heat lightning lit up the trail before us. A continuous series pulsed the rest of the way back to the barn, the rain holding off until we got there.

This was my Saul Experience. Thankfully, God did not have to blind me and knock me off my horse to get my attention! The gentle flashes of heat lightning in the distance were enough. They suggested that illumination about a particular situation might come from an unexpected source. In addition, the impending rain and its eventual arrival suggested that an answer to a prayer was on its way. I felt very comforted.

Our second night ride was inspired by September's full moon. I wanted to experience moonrise on Highlander. We took the same trail as before, again leaving at dusk. There was no heat lightning this time, so the woods seemed darker. Like tiny luminaries, firefly larvae lit the shores of the last stream crossing. I smiled at the subtlety of this source of illumination. Soon afterward, Highlander and I found ourselves walking toward a glowing, orange ball peeking above the hilly horizon. After some twists and turns of the trail, the rising moon backlit the rest of our return to the barn.

This was my Metaphor Experience. God is Light and, as such, is everywhere—from the glow of a tiny firefly to the glow of a large full moon.

Highlander and I took a different trail on our third night ride. The woods got really dark this time. Fortunately, I had saved the widest stretch for the way home; however, by the time we arrived, this "wide stretch" had shrunk to a thin ribbon that was all I could discern in the dark, and discernment took total concentration. What luxury for a teacher, exhausted from multitasking, only to have one thing to do and no distractions!

This was my Zen Experience. God seemed to be telling me to simplify my life by not taking on so much. I was reminded to stay present in the moment instead of reliving the past or planning the future.

Further illumination about the significance of my night rides arrived during a student's Bat Mitzvah ceremony. The young lady had chosen to speak on Isaiah 60:19 and 20. The words stunned me: "No longer shall you need the sun for light by day nor the shining of the moon for radiance by night; for the Lord shall be your light everlasting, your God shall be your glory. Your sun shall set no more, your moon no more withdraw, for the Lord shall be a light to you forever. . ."

Her rabbi's recounting of 1st Kings 19:11-12 really resonated, too. It's the verse about God not being in the roaring wind, the earthquake, or the fire, but in the still, small voice within. What I more fully realized was that riding is a sacred activity, a way of praying, of praising God for creation, of withdrawing from the busyness of my life, and of creating the silence necessary to hear God.

And I'm never alone when I ride. Not only am I with God, I'm with the angel in horsehair that God has sent me! I am truly blessed. I'm glad it's cool out now because I can wear my new sweatshirt. It proclaims, "Horses are proof that God loves us and wants us to be happy." Amen!

November, 2003. Original version published in The Trail Rider, January/February, 2004

CHAPTER 15
THANK YOU, GOD!

By this time, Dancer was in full retirement and had joined Highlander at his stable. A special thanks to Reverend Alta for coming out to bless both horses.

Thank you, God, for:

- the return of spring and enough daylight to visit the stable again after work

- the greetings of Highlander and Dancer, my two very favorite horses in the whole wide world

- Dancer walking right over for his carrot and Highlander dramatically taking his good old time

- Highlander neighing good-bye to Dancer as he and I head for the trails

- unwinding after a hectic day in the peaceful evening woods

- my beloved steed rocking me with the meditative rhythm of his walk

- visiting the Cathedral of the Pine Forest for the first time since last November

- feeling God's presence so strongly there that an exclamation of praise bursts from my mouth
- Highlander neighing "I'm home" to Dancer upon our return
- Dancer nickering a soft "welcome back" in reply

March, 2004

Chapter 16
THE METAPHYSICS OF INSECTS

Each October, I teach insects to my fifth-grade science class. My students net, observe, and release insects outdoors, then create models of them for classroom display. This year, the unit was interrupted by two days of parent conferences. During the second-to-last conference, a parent made a stinging remark. I tried hard not to react but was still burning the next day—a picture-perfect fall Saturday—while riding through the woods.

My mood further declined when a few small gnats began swarming around my helmeted head. Fixated upon them, I swatted the air with increasing frustration. In my myopic state, I was oblivious of the colorful trees and unable to enjoy my inaugural ride in my new saddle. Worst of all, I lost communion with my horse.

Unfortunately, I repeated the same behavior the next morning. And, once again, insects pointed out my error.

After looking forward all week to riding with my former endurance mentor, I had arrived at the barn only to discover that my horse's back was somewhat sore. Because Susan had trailered her horse so far to meet me, I accompanied her on a short ride. Instead of enjoying another beautiful day off and her company, however, I struggled unsuccessfully to eliminate the black thoughts swarming through my head. My new saddle wasn't the solution to my intensive two-year search to cure my horse's back problem, and it was embarrassing that I had a chronically sore horse.

Certified the year before as an equine massage therapist, I knew the importance of correct saddle fit. My misguided previous assumption that a saddle fits when the girth reaches around the horse's middle, much like watch straps around one's wrist, had been corrected: It is imperative that a saddle aligns with the contour of a horse's back. I had responsibly tried out different friends' saddles and narrowed my choice to one of Jonesy's. I'd carefully traced Highlander's back, ordered a custom saddle of the same make and model, and sold my two used saddles to finance the majority of its cost.

Yet Highlander's back was still sore. He clearly needed an expensive chiropractic adjustment. I didn't own the truck and trailer necessary to transport him to a chiropractor. I needed to make more money. . .

These downward-spiraling images came to an abrupt halt when angry yellow jackets suddenly swarmed out of a hole in the ground and attacked Susan and her horse. Both, stung repeatedly, were clearly in pain. We needed to return to her trailer for some first aid.

It wasn't until church that afternoon that I realized I had reacted to the parent comment much like I had reacted to the gnats. Instead of letting the insignificance drift away, I had not only held onto it, I had blown it out of proportion by focusing so much energy upon it. And, because I had chosen to dwell on one negative experience instead of the majority of positive parent comments, not only had I suffered, I had increased my pain!

The next time my thinking darkens. I will remember what the insects taught me last weekend. Their first alert was delivered by a few harmless gnats. Their second, borne by an angry swarm of predatory wasps, had escalated substantially in intensity. I don't want to risk the severity of a third communiqué!

* * *

Post Script: I ended up employing Kelly's services. A certified saddle fitter, he re-measured Highlander's back and went shopping with me. The very first store had two saddles that fit Highlander's back. The better-fitting one was the same make and model as the offending saddle that I was trading in! Apparently, my measuring skills hadn't been up to par because it only fit Highlander in front, whereas the model on sale fit him in both the front and the back. But it was tagged 'sold.' Fortunately, the second saddle was almost new (and I'm still using it).

Kelly has had an interesting career. He started out as a pediatric physical therapist. While working with children enrolled in a hippotherapy program at a riding stable, he observed that the horses needed some therapy of their own. He obtained certifications as an equine massage therapist, an English saddle stuffer, a saddle fitter, and an equine chiropractor. Combining aspects of his varied background, Kelly has created a unique form of equine body work.

October, 2004

CHAPTER 17
THANKS, MOM!

One June evening, Highlander and I went for a quick jog. It was still warm out, but much cooler and less humid than the afternoon. An intense thunder, lightning, and rain storm exploded and quickly spent itself.

I didn't realize that the trees were still wet until we turned off the gravel fire road and onto a dirt single track; every time we bumped a branch, Highlander and I were generously sprinkled! I was immediately transported back to Mass at my Catholic grade school—the priest was casting a watery blessing in my direction with his wand-like aspergil. Getting splashed, both then and now, was fun!

By the time the trail looped back to the road, my clothes were quite damp. Our long trot to the barn was refreshingly cool. As my clothes dried, I again reverted to childhood. I was home on ironing day (Tuesday). My mother, with her sprinkling bottle in hand—a blue Tupperware tumbler with a clear, perforated, snap-on lid—was moistening a piece of clothing. Washed and hung out to dry the previous day (laundry day), it now lay on the silver, scorch-proof cover of her ironing board. As soon as the item absorbed the proper amount of water, she rolled it up and piled it atop the other dampened items awaiting her heating iron.

I thought of all the weeks, months, and years that Mom had shopped for, purchased, washed, ironed, and put away my clothes. Suddenly, after decades of doing these tasks (but a lot less ironing) on my own, I realized what a huge blessing she had bestowed upon me and how I had totally taken her services for granted. Thanks, Mom!

June, 2005

Chapter 18
Instant Messaging

One evening after work, I had only limited time to ride. So instead of staying on the graveled fire road back to the barn, I took a single-track short cut. I prefer the narrow dirt paths still exclusively reserved for horse traffic. On them, I feel immersed in a living forest rather than an outsider observing a still life. I also like the whimsy of single tracks. Originally straight, they are now loop-de-loop. As trees fell across them over the years, riders rode around them, thus creating the curves.

Highlander and I started tracing a new curve when we came upon a recently-downed tree. Navigating around it was a challenge at first—he wanted to rush through the dense undergrowth, while I, not wanting to scrape off a body part, puncture an eye, or get whipped by a gauntlet of branches, wanted him to pick his way through slowly and carefully. Once he understood that, we safely maneuvered our way back to the trail. We reached the barn as darkness descended.

The following Saturday afternoon, we took the same short-cut but in the opposite direction. When we reached the newly fallen tree, we were unable to discern the tracing of our original bypass. As we negotiated over, around, and through stickers, vines, uneven ground, and rafts of fallen limbs, I lost my sense of direction. We began following a dry stream bed, but soon found it barricaded by a hopeless tangle of fallen trees. I felt as if we were small pawns in a chaotic pile of giant Pick-up sticks.

After going up and down a few hills in various directions, I was totally disoriented.

I wasn't too concerned, as we had ridden this part of the woods for years and were in no real danger—the weather was good, it would be light for hours yet, and we were certain to stumble upon one of the several trails crisscrossing the area—but we had to be careful. If we misstepped and got hurt, the stable owners would have difficulty finding us. Wanting to get back to the barn on time, I prayed aloud for guidance. As soon as I uttered my last word, I heard human voices wafting through the woods.

I yelled, "Hi, can you hear me?" and heard a comforting "Yes" in reply.

"Are you on horses?"

"Yes."

"On a trail?"

"Yes."

"I'm on a chestnut and we're temporarily lost. Will you stop and wait where you are while we follow your voices?"

"Yes."

When Highlander and I got to the trail, we were greeted by the six angels God had sent to our rescue—one man, two women, and three horses. They told us what trail we were on and exactly where we were on it.

To me, because prayer had trumped technology—I never had to so much as remove my cell phone from my fanny pack—GPS now stands for God's Prayer Service!

August, 2005

CHAPTER 19
MY HERO

Sometime later, on another midweek evening ride along the same trail, Highlander and I got into another predicament. As we started down a short slope, we came upon a skinny-trunked tree which had fallen across the trail. No problem; Highlander easily stepped over it. A few feet later, we came to a fallen tree with a much wider trunk. Highlander had to step higher to clear it. And some yards beyond, we were intercepted by a medium-trunked downed tree, both of its ends obstructed by thick undergrowth. Figuring that more storm damage most likely lay ahead, I decided to cut our ride short and head back to the barn. It was almost dusk, and we didn't have time to navigate a challenging obstacle course.

Highlander happily did a quick turn on the forehand, but this time the widest trunk, now on the uphill slope, stopped him in his tracks. It was way too high for him to step over from below, and jumping it successfully would require considerable luck, even if there had been a long enough "runway" behind us to build up the required speed.

I took a deep breath and dismounted. The trunk looked even higher from the ground, but, before getting out my cell phone to ask someone to bring out a chain saw, I wanted to try something.

I unsnapped the reins from Highlander's halter-bridle and attached one end to his chin strap, thus making a long lead rope. Then I climbed over the log, stood to his left, and told him, "If you think you can jump this log without hurting yourself—it should be easier without my weight—you're going to have to do it. Otherwise, you'll be eating dinner a bit later than usual tonight. You can do it, boy!" After thinking for a second, Highlander pushed off with his hind legs—from a standstill!—and raised the front part of his body up and over the trunk.

He was now straddled across it, and it was touching his belly. Assuming that he was now hopelessly stuck, I reached for my cell phone. Quick as a wink, Highlander—again, from a standstill!—bucked up his back legs and set them on top of the fallen tree trunk. Then he pushed off, clearing both it and the small fallen tree in front of it!

I could hardly believe what I had seen! My hero, by using his brain and his brawn, had saved the day!

Story's insertion point guesstimated

CHAPTER 20
FLYING RIBBONS

Highlander and I celebrated the weather-perfect day before Derby *in* "the oaks" together. The Oaks is the filly race the day before The Kentucky Derby at Churchill Downs. We started our ride on a gravel trail that doubles for a few furlongs as a family's driveway. The elder son was heading toward us on his mountain bike. When he got close, he politely stopped to avoid scaring Highlander, allowing us to safely pass him.

After a pleasant chat, Highlander and I entered a green woods, salted with white multiflora rose, blackberry, locust, and daisy fleabane flowers. A beautiful blue sky peeked through the canopy above.

The plastic ribbons marking the course of last week's endurance ride were still hanging intermittently from the branches of the trees, serving as markers. I reached over to remove them as we passed. To avoid littering, I tied them to the straps between Highlander's breast collar and saddle—the fluorescent pink ribbons to the right and the fluorescent yellow ones to the left. When we got as far as my schedule permitted, we turned around and headed back to the barn. It was feeding time, so Highlander launched into a brisk trot. The ribbons tied to his tack took flight. Suddenly, I was a young girl racing on my bicycle again. The multi-colored streamers on the ends of my handlebars were flat out horizontal and snapping like whips. In my young imagination, the metal skeleton beneath me had morphed into a flesh and blood horse, its mane and tail flying in the wind as we galloped along.

That dream was now reality!

May, 2005. Original version published in Endurance News, November, 2006

CHAPTER 21
NOT THE EXPECTED ANSWER TO MY PRAYER

I thought I'd found the perfect antidote to my developing teacher burnout: winning a spa vacation, including life coaching, in an Oprah contest. I'd carefully composed my application, mailed it, and confidently awaited my acceptance, only to find out that I wasn't one of the 50 winners. How could this be, when I had felt such strong inner guidance to apply? Although it was very windy, I was compelled to ride Highlander and demand an explanation from God. Here is the reply I received:

Dear Jan,

Notice where you are right now—stirred up emotionally and riding Highlander in the wind. Yet, you feel perfectly calm. You have complete faith in his steadiness. Your trust in him is the result of the many years you have spent building your relationship.

Despite your tendency to worry, you are not the least bit concerned about Highlander bolting, pitching you off, or abandoning you. Nor are you worried about a tree—or, with your imagination, the entire forest—falling on you, pinning you down, or knocking you out.

So why is it that when you are in the midst of mental and emotional storms, you don't always consider and trust in MY presence?

Right now, feel Highlander carrying you. Really feel him. Memorize his feel—his stability, his strength, his forward motion.

Listen to his whinny when you get back to the barn. As you rub him down, smell his sweat. Feel his warmth and his softness. Notice his size and also his gentleness. Enjoy the tickle of his breath and the velvet of his muzzle when you feed him his carrot. See yourself reflected in his large, luminous eyes and get lost in their infinity.

Recall these things when you next need to feel my presence. I am now and will always be as close to you as Highlander is at this very moment. You already possess a great prize.

Love, God

Post Script: Once, I was asked to close my eyes, focus them on the space in between, and notice what I "saw." What appeared was a big, moist, horse eye, fringed with long lashes.

February, 2007

CHAPTER 22
ABUNDANT WEALTH

When I'm consumed with feelings of lack, I know it's time to hop on my horse and head for the woods. Once there, it doesn't take me long to shift my focus to abundance. During the summer, I think of the infinity of green leaves as bills, each species a different denomination. I imagine the leaves neatly bundled in trunk-like stacks that dwarf us.

When the leaves turn color in the fall, I pretend that the yellow ones are coins of the purest gold, loosely piled like the Knobs of Indiana.

On white, winter days, I imagine the snow crystals reflecting the sun as glittering diamonds. On snowless days, I focus on the rocks and exposed tree roots covered with fluorescent green moss—they are huge chunks of priceless emeralds and jade. In the spring, each flower and leaf bud represents the promise of a blessing in my life beginning to unfold.

These meditations help me shift my thoughts and emotions. Not only does gratitude feel a whole lot better than lack, it attracts more riches.

Thank God for the visionaries who preserved public properties with trails for me to ride upon.

March, 2007

CHAPTER 23
NOT ONE, BUT THREE SIGNS

To this old work horse, the pasture is looking greener and greener on the other side of the fence. To teach or not to teach—I'd poured my all into teaching for 30 years and was becoming increasingly restless. I wanted a sign—an unmistakable one accompanied by lightning, fireworks, and blinking neon lights—indicating what I should do. In a grand cosmic joke, I ended up getting not one, but three signs. Literally.

The first two came last fall. I was driving my routine route home from the stable after riding. First, my attention was drawn to the "Stop" sign at a 3-way intersection. Second, I saw the "Limit 30" sign just beyond it. Okay—I was supposed to stop teaching. And, pray tell, do what?

Fear struck. Obviously, I would need another job. But what else could I do besides teach? Nothing I like to do pays well. Would anyone hire a 55-year-old? Would I get retirement and health care? Would I be able to fit in enough time for riding? My heart and my head wrestled all winter. My head said to keep teaching. My heart said I needed to move on.

In the spring, I got my third sign. "Slow, Children Playing" was near the same 3-way, across from a church. I understood the "slow"—getting some rest sounded wonderful—but the recess reference escaped me. Perhaps it meant that my new job was supposed to be so enjoyable that it didn't seem like work. Hmmm . . . what career had I envisioned as a child? Cowgirl;

National Geographic Explorer-Journalist; veterinarian. Instead, I'd fallen into teaching—I'm the eldest child in my family, had done a fair share of babysitting, had always been a serious student, and liked to help people. . .

Back to playing . . . what did I play as a kid? Games like SPUD; hide and seek; jump rope (regular, with some Chinese and Double Dutch thrown in); tag (all sorts, butterfly being my favorite); Red Rover; Simon Says; board games; Mass (with potato chips or Necco Wafers for Communion); Cowboys and Indians (I preferred being an Indian); and school. Instead of dolls, I played with stuffed animals, wishing I could cast a spell and bring them to life. . .

The urge to work and play with animals is resurfacing. I don't know how things will work out, but I see a gate opening and feel a growing urge to step out of my familiar pasture!

Between fall, 2006 and spring, 2007

CHAPTER 24
MY PROFESSIONAL RETIREMENT

After 30 years of teaching science, 24 at the same school, I decided to retire. More introverted than extraverted, I had finally burned all the way out and wanted to spend time exploring other areas of interest I'd never had enough time or energy for.

I always enjoyed the last teachers' meeting of the year. The students were off for the summer, most of our work was done, and it was time for the faculty and staff to kick back and enjoy each other's company. After lunch, thoughtful and creative awards and honors were given to those who had completed their first, fifth, tenth, fifteenth, etc. year of service and to those retiring.

Legend had it that, one year, a retiree departed the luncheon in a hot air balloon. I, myself, witnessed a proper southern lady, clinging to the Head of Maintenance, speed off on a motorcycle. For once, I wanted to make a splash, too, instead of staying comfortably in the background.

During my tenure, I'd twice been pressed to participate in school assemblies starring lip-synching teachers—once as Cher singing "I Got You Babe" with a male drama teacher, and once as Nancy Sinatra, voicing "These Boots are Made for Walking" to the head master and two male teachers. Despite my nerves, I hadn't fainted, and the audience had gone wild—one colleague told me she wished she'd been wearing diapers! So I hatched my exit plan and began making arrangements.

The day of the luncheon, everything went according to plan. My husband had taken off a few hours from work to attend, and Dixie, a friend with a horse trailer, had transported Highlander and Wannettia to school. The trailer was parked outside the glass-enclosed lunchroom and Highlander was tied to it, happily munching grass. I was in my costume—riding boots and tights partially hidden by a lab coat, its pockets containing a pair of safety goggles and a pair of plastic gloves. The two colleagues acting as DJs had obtained and queued my music selection.

I was the last honoree, so everyone was finished eating by the time my turn came. Two fellow science teachers (one of whom I'd taught as an 8th-grader) gave speeches about me—one serious and one funny—and presented me with a lovely scrapbook depicting special memories during my years of service. At their conclusion, my recording began.

I quickly donned my gloves and goggles and stood up to begin my solo performance. As the "da-da-ta-das" of David Rose's "The Stripper" rose in volume, I wove through the tables, slowly, and one at a time, removing goggles and gloves and throwing each into different areas of the audience. After unbuttoning and dispensing with my lab coat, I led everyone outside to meet Highlander. I quickly tacked him up, mounted, and rode into the figurative sunset.

We were paralleling the state highway in front of the school when a bus from a school still in session passed. Children were leaving their school for the day as I was leaving mine for good. At the end of the campus, Highlander and I turned left, passed by the sports fields, and then entered the nature preserve where my students and I had made so many interesting discoveries over the years—and in which I had always wanted to ride.

Post Script: I soon found a part time job at a kennel. Brownie, the stuffed dog of my childhood, had finally came alive; and, instead of taking human children out for recess, I was now taking him and his buddies outside.

May, 2007

Chapter 25
NIGHT LIGHTS

One cool evening at the end of a heat wave, Highlander and I left for a leisurely ride through the woods. Darkness found us blissfully trotting the sinuous trail in the valley—until we reached the lone clearing.

There, the orange-glowing, jack-o-lantern grin of a huge, low, waxing crescent moon stopped us in our tracks. Near it, slightly above a pond, a gigantic dipper sparkled in suspended animation.

Had it just drawn some water out or poured some water in?

August, 2007

CHAPTER 26
FALL BOUNTY

The afternoon was cool but pleasant—the wind intermittent, the sky clear, and the sun shining. Highlander and I were patrolling the trails for litter. Along the ridge, yellow leaves rained upon us like manna from heaven, and rainwater sparkled like diamonds in the curled leaves mulching the trail.

At the bottom of the long, steep descent, we saw two hikers. Before we overtook them, they turned off the multi-use trail and onto a hiking trail. Highlander and I continued on the multi-use trail.

As soon as we crossed a dry stream bed, I spotted a Styrofoam "peanut" hanging from a signless rebar stake on the left. I plucked the tidbit off and was placing it in my plastic grocery bag when a voice pronounced, "That's mine."

I looked over my shoulder expecting to see the hikers, but neither was there. The voice repeated, "That's mine." On second thought, I mused, perhaps the voice had come from on high. Wondering exactly what he was referring to—the manna or the diamonds—I looked up and saw God, convincingly manifesting as a hunter in full camouflage, in a dear stand.

He added, "Doe urine."

Not at all comprehending his message, I eloquently replied, "Huh?"

He repeated, "Doe urine."

Still not understanding this totally unanticipated divine message, I again mumbled, "Huh?"

"That thing you just picked up—it's doe urine, and you can just toss it under this tree."

Fumbling to retrieve the packing chip from my plastic bag, I collected myself enough to string together a few words. "I'm picking up litter," I stammered.

As we moved on, he blessed us with a polite, "Thank you." I was so relieved to receive his approval!

A few twists and turns down the trail, a third form of prosperity appeared—a quarter moon hanging in the sky next to the round, slowly-setting sun.

Manna, diamonds, coins, and a message from above—not a bad haul for one day!

November, 2008

CHAPTER 27
BREATHE!

Thoughts were busily whirling in my mind when Highlander stopped suddenly on the trail. I knew him too well to urge him forward; he was trying to tell me something, but what? That a horse and rider were around the bend? That a deer or a wild turkey was in the brush? That he needed to relieve himself?

No, no, and no. But what did he mean? Eventually, I got his message. This January day was his first time out of the pasture since deer hunting season late last fall, and he was taking in the forest again.

While he looked around curiously and smelled the changes in the air, I was just supposed to sit and breathe . . . deep breaths, conscious breaths, slow and even breaths.

As I inhaled and exhaled, my attention shifted from thinking to feeling. First, there was the wind—cool and moderate, with a hint of spring. Then, there were Highlander's ribs, rhythmically expanding and contracting beneath me, setting a calming cadence for the pumping of my lungs.

The wind was the breath of God surrounding me, and Highlander was the support of God grounding me. A holy moment!

January, 2009

63

CHAPTER 28
GODSPEED, DEAR PEGASUS

In January, four months shy of his 31st birthday, Dancer's spirit entered the white light on its flight home to The Maker.

In March, a new endurance rider asked to ride with me. We met in a department store parking lot, I in my car and she in her truck, trailer in tow. As I led the way up the interstate to Highlander's stable, vehicles streamed past us, and an old-fashioned white delivery truck cut into the slow lane in front of me. Time stood still when I noticed the black painting on its back. As soon as "The Pegasus Company" and a circle around a winged horse registered in my brain, the truck pulled back into the passing lane and disappeared into faster traffic.

Had Dancer sent me a message? Did the logo's circle intimate a new link in an ever-growing chain (the delivery truck = Dancer, my car = me, and the rig behind me = a newbie to distance riding)? Did the highway symbolize the progression of life—that it's time for me to pass on what I've learned about the trails and the sport?

Was the long-distance champ, who, I think, had communicated long distance to me twice when he was alive, now saying that, after having granted me time to grieve, he needed to move on? All I know for sure is that I finally felt at peace.

* * *

On July 9th, Marshall, co-owner of the stable, and I planted a redbud sapling—the purple-leaved variety—on Dancer's grave.

Valentines dancing in the breeze seemed a fitting marker for the horse who'd always set my heart aflutter.

* * *

Dancer's Streak
5/2/1978-1/29/09
Godspeed, dear Pegasus, until we meet again.

CHAPTER 29
CATHARSIS

I LOVE to ride both in warm rain and at night. Both private experiences give my restless soul a deep sense of peace.

I've always enjoyed thunderstorms too—the promise of long-building, pent-up moodiness finally and dramatically releasing, then being replaced by deep calm. So often, these storms mirror my emotions.

Although I usually watch thunderstorms through the windows of a building, I enjoy them more from inside an open barn. The best vantage point, however, is on the trail during warm weather.

Once, when I was feeling particularly out-of-sorts, the emotional storm within me melded with the atmospheric one surrounding me. My feelings transformed into salty tears just as the humidity exploded into a downpour. I got cleansed inside and out at the same time. It was a delicious—primitive, yet sacramental—moment.

NOTE: I avoid riding during lightning storms and high winds.

Story's insertion-point guesstimated

CHAPTER 30
I CAN PICK UP LITTER!

*L*ent, 2009, found me looking for a service to perform. The litter on the horse trails bothered me—it not only spoiled the view, it baffled me because I believe that God graced us with the beauty of nature and public lands to enjoy and care for, not to deface. To me, tossing litter anywhere but into a garbage can is as unthinkable as tossing it onto an altar. So I decided to pick up litter every time I rode during the Lenten season.

Lent came and went, and Highlander and I had only made a dent in cleaning the trails. I pushed myself out of my comfort zone and solicited help, eventually coordinating with a few other litter-picker-uppers I met over the next few years. While we never eradicated the litter problem, we contributed towards its solution, and I think God was pleased.

I used to feel inferior to my endurance friends who live in the country and clear the horse trails after big storms. Armed with thick, clanking chains and hungry saws, they mount their horses, ATVs, tractors, or backhoes, and head out to remove downed trees and limbs. A few times I followed along to drag off the branches and small logs they left in their wake. Wanting to upgrade my lowly status afterwards, I committed to picking up litter every time I rode. It was a job anyone could do—or so I first thought.

Today, for example—instead of saddle bags, I took only a plastic grocery bag with me when I went riding. I didn't expect to encounter much litter as I was going to ride portions of the route my friend Gretchen and I had cleaned less than two weeks ago.

At first, all went well. The only trash was the dumped tire I'd already reported to the state property managers. My hopes were rising. Maybe today would be the day I had been dreaming about, the day the trails would be garbage-free, the day I would be totally able to enjoy the scenery, the day I would not have to stress my horse's back nor my saddle with continuous dismounting and remounting.

This delusion soon evaporated. By the time Highlander and I reached the gate marking the end of the trail on our side and the end of a car pull-off on the opposite roadside, my bag was half full. I dismounted to remove the trash that had accumulated nearby.

I left the paper napkin piled with human feces to biodegrade, but picked up the bandana, its classy horse motif now spoiled with "residue" from some wiping. (Yes, I was wearing gloves, and yes, I washed them and the bandana as soon as I got home.)

The surrounding litter wasn't as nasty, but it was more difficult to extract. Some was in mud, some in puddles, some partially buried in the ground, and some in brambles. Some was probably even in poison ivy, but it being almost winter and there being no leaves to identify, I couldn't tell. Trying my best to hold onto a 1,200-pound horse fixated on a nearby grassy patch, I dove into some thorns to extricate a few aluminum cans, plastic bottles, and Styrofoam cups—unthinkingly taking the bag with me. It, of course, got slashed in several places, and most of its hard-gained contents spilled out. After picking everything back up and wrapping them as best I could in the torn plastic, I led Highlander down the road toward some houses in hopes of finding a new bag donor. No one was out. No sooner had I given up the cause, turned around, and remounted, than a passing motorist stopped. It was Wanda, who had recently moved into the farm across from Highlander's stable.

My normally trusty mount, who usually puts up with litter collection obligingly, chose that moment to protest that he had had more than enough of the activity. It was cold out, it was feeding time, and he wanted to go home—immediately and directly. He worked himself into a tizzy—probably enticing Wanda to seriously reconsider my invitation to ride together soon—as she started walking over to us with two new bags. At first, I thought she was being extra nice by throwing in the free delivery, but concluded she was probably trying to protect her vehicle from my now-spinning horse. I used one bag for the litter I'd picked up and saved the second one for our return to the stable. Wanda (yes, I forewarned her about its contents) volunteered to take the full bag home to her trash can. She also offered to dispose of any additional trash I picked up—I just had to drop it off at her mailbox. I gratefully promised to do so, and she drove off.

Highlander interpreted her departure as an invitation to race. It was all I could do to turn him off the road and back onto the now-clean horse trail where—fortunately, in private—he went into full-scale rebellion. He took off at top speed with me standing in my stirrups, pulling his reins and S hackamore with my entire body weight. I eventually convinced him that we were heading directly home (silly boy)! He made a few half-hearted bucks to emphasize his displeasure at continued litter pick up, but he slowed to a sane pace.

I, however, had a new bag to fill. So I soon turned him onto a different trail to the barn, stopping every now and then to remove more litter. We were almost back when we came upon a fallen tree across the trail and had to ride through some brambles to maneuver around it. When we got back to the trail, I looked down to check on the bag, only to find that I was just holding handles. Once again, I dismounted and picked up the litter. I wrapped it as best I could in the torn remnants of the severed bag. My grasp was so tenuous, there was no way I could maintain it while mounting. So with one hand holding the litter and the other holding the reins, I led Highlander home.

As I walked, my full-length chaps started to fall down. Today was the first time this year that I'd zipped them over my riding tights for warmth, and I hadn't belted them snuggly enough. Both of my hands being full, my attempts to pull up the chaps were clumsy, and I ended up with a wedgie I couldn't undo.

Back at the stable, I freed my underwear, untacked and turned Highlander out, rebagged and carried the fresh trash to Wanda's mailbox, and jumped into my car. As soon as I got home, I dashed to the bathroom to wash my hands (several times). The mirror revealed several trickles of blood on my face, the result of my bramble encounters.

I feel a whole lot better about myself these days. Some of my horsey friends may be able to drive ATVs and wield chainsaws, but me? I can pick up litter!

November, 2009

CHAPTER 31
THE GIFT THAT KEEPS ON GIVING

Mother's Day, 2010: I began thinking about Dancer while gazing at *"Spring Morn,"* a print of a large Paul Detlefsen painting that my husband and I hang in our living room each year when winter ends.

I've always loved the picture. The white horse reminds me of Dancer and the redbud trees in the woods where I ride. This year, however, the juxtaposition of the horse and the flowering redbud in the grassy pasture along the creek grabbed me. I hadn't thought about the painting when I'd chosen to mark Dancer's grave behind his pasture with a redbud tree, but perhaps it had been my subconscious motivation?

I imagined Dancer in heaven enjoying his well-deserved, eternal rest. He is young and healthy, grazing with a full set of perfect teeth on fresh grass in an abundant pasture with a never-ending supply of fresh drinking water. The weather is always perfect and the air always pure.

Psalm 23:1-3 sprang to mind: *"The Lord is my shepherd, I shall not want. He makes me lie down in green pastures; He leads me beside quiet waters. He restores my soul…"*

* * *

Fall, 2011: My six-year search has ended! I've finally located a braider within driving distance willing to teach me how to make a horsehair bracelet!

I'd become aware of braided horsehair jewelry six years ago on a trail ride with Jonesey. She showed me a bracelet she'd purchased during a vacation out West; I was instantly captivated and determined to learn how to make a bracelet for myself.

* * *

Spring, 2012: One morning, I got up early and drove several hours to the braider's home in an adjoining state. A four-hour afternoon lesson felt like an initiation into a secret club I'd long quested to join. Afterwards, I began the long process of practicing and honing my new skills.

My first bracelet was a spiral-patterned, 4-string braid made from Dancer's white tail hair and the all-red hairs I had patiently pulled out from the multi-colored swatch I'd cut from the underside of Highlander's dock. I made a necklace to match, and on it hung a carved and polished cedar heart. This simple set of jewelry is one of my favorite possessions.

2010-2012

CHAPTER 32
GONE

For the ten years that Jim and I owned Highlander, our horse hadn't so much as set a hoof in a ring or received any formal training—nor, to my knowledge, had he ever. So to celebrate my 60th birthday, I thought it would be fun to send him to a trainer for two months. After Nate worked Highlander for a couple weeks in the indoor arena, he gave us lessons together. They concentrated on gaiting (my half-Tennessee Walker naturally trotted), the canter, side passing, and an obstacle challenge. I thoroughly enjoyed our education.

During it, Marshall and Wannettia decided to close their boarding business. I had to find a new stable to move Highlander to when our time was up at Nate's. I chose one near a trailhead in the lowlands to their south and closer to my home.

Soon after moving Highlander to his new stable, Gretchen and I planned to meet at Wanda and Ray's (across from the old stable). I was going to buy some hay that Gretchen had volunteered to truck down to Highlander. When the weather forecast—not good to begin with—got increasingly worse, we decided to reschedule.

Thus, Gretchen and I weren't present when an EF4 tornado struck the area. The couples mentioned above sustained minor hail and wind damage, but David, our friend across the ridge, was not so fortunate. The tornado touched down on his property, essentially robbing him of everything he owned, including his horses. The one exception, and only comfort, was the survival of his elderly—and much traumatized—cat, who had gotten trapped in a dresser drawer which itself had gotten stuck in his small cellar. David was alive solely because the tornado occurred on a Friday during work hours, and he wasn't home.

Jim, Gretchen, and I joined the large group of David's friends who gathered the next day to remove debris from his pastures. The devastation of the tornado was sobering—worse than it looked on TV and worse than we'd imagined—a fearsome demonstration of Mother Nature's power.

David's house was gone, including all but a few of the huge, hand hewn, pre-Civil War timbers that had formed its core. The remaining few timbers had been uncoupled and tossed hither and yon like toothpicks. David's barn and fences were gone, along with his truck and horse trailer. A bare, concrete barn pad marked his missing homestead.

The forest between Highlander's old stable and David's place was gone. One-half of its rim used to be on the ridge and the other half in the valley below. Now the bowl of forest was empty. The loss was heartbreaking. The lovely, winding, wooded trail cradled within, a trail that Highlander and I had ridden for years—actually, my favorite trail in the area, one that had inspired so many of my horse tales and from which I'd picked up litter—had vanished. Left behind was acre upon acre of tilted, topless trees and a brown, lifeless, post-apocalyptic vista as far as the eye could see.

The area was closed for over a year for logging and public safety. When it reopened, it was an ugly, dry, and scarred hellhole totally exposed to the sun—a depressingly far cry from its former glory.

My heart was torn—half grateful that Highlander and I had escaped the tornado's wrath and now had the unscathed southern trails to ride, and half broken for David and his beloved lost herd.

**May you rest in peace,
Vamos (colt), Vivace (dam), Miss Vivaldi (grand-dam),
Gabriella, Bode, and Czoya**

Post Script: *David eventually rebuilt and got back into horses.*

March 2, 2012

CHAPTER 33
RANGE RIDER

I was so excited! Jim and I were taking our first longer-than-a-weekend vacation since our honeymoon at Mackinaw Island. It was early summer, and we were going out West to visit friends of his whom I'd never met and who owned horses!

Day One—we left the Louisville Airport (501 feet above sea level) and arrived at the Denver Airport (5,430 feet).

Day Two—we acclimatized to the Mile High City by taking in some of the exhibitions at the impressive Museum of Nature and Science. Jim and I started off together, then divided up to explore on our own. I, a second generation American of Eastern European descent, was drawn to North American Indian cultures. As long as I can remember, I've been fascinated by their affinity for horses and their harmony with nature. It's intriguing how humans of all early cultures used native materials—plants, clay, bones, hides, shells, rocks, horsehair, porcupine quills, etc.—not only to make daily necessities but also to create awe-inspiring works of art. The displays were fantastic and the artifacts interesting, but it was the simple, long rope made of horsehair that spoke to me most.

Day Three—Jim and I took a leisurely drive to Golden (5,675 feet) and overnighted there to further improve our altitude adjustment.

Day Four—we took a roller coaster ride. We climbed the Rocky Mountains to the Eisenhower/Johnson Memorial Tunnel (the highest vehicle tunnel in the world) just below the Berthoud Pass (11,307 feet) in Colorado's Continental Divide. Then we dipped to the town of Silverthorne (9,035 feet), hopped up to Rabbit Ears Pass (9,426 feet), and slipped down to a ski resort town (6,732 feet) in the Yampa Valley.

For hundreds of years, the valley had served as the summer hunting ground of the Ute Indians and its many mineral springs as medicine for Ute and Arapaho tribes seeking physical and spiritual healing. Around 1800, French trappers tracked the incongruous sound of a steamboat chugging along a river to a bubbling spring. By the turn of the century, a town was built around and named for the geothermal hot spot.

It was at the library in Steamboat, across the parking lot from that very spring, where we met up with our hosts, Terry and Gerry. The couple led us to their nearby home in a land conservation community on a former cattle ranch in the foothills of the Park Range. Its 1700 acres are divided into 35 ten-acre lots. The remainder, which abuts State land as well as that of the Bureau of Land Management lands, serves as a commons for conservation and recreation. After introducing us to their house pets, Terry and Gerry took us out to meet their two horses, Eclipse and Midnight Dancer. Dancer, a Tennessee Walker with black and white paint coloring, was to be my mount during our stay! That evening, Gerry took me out for my first-ever ride on a gaited horse. I'd heard that gaited horses give smoother rides than trotters and was eager to experience the difference. Dancer was a sweetheart and her movement a treat. Apparently, because she always has three feet on the ground (her gait is a four-beat movement), she avoids Highlander's rise and fall during the trot (a two-beat movement) and the canter (a three-beat movement) when more than one foot is in the air.

Days Five through Seven—Terry and Gerry were consummate hosts, and the next three days of our visit fell into a routine.

One or the other rode with me after breakfast, and later on all four of us went into town to try out a restaurant and explore. We visited the local historical museum, a Western apparel store (in front of which we met a living, breathing longhorn), and the impressive, volunteer-created-and-run botanical gardens.

The weather was perfect—sunny and warm with low humidity, a refreshing change from the sticky heat of Southern Indiana. The trails were heavenly—bugless, dirt, and private one-tracks. The hills were less steep and rocky than some in the Knobs of Southeastern Indiana that overlook the Ohio River and downtown Louisville.

The ranch's valleys and foothills were grassy and dotted with ponds serving as drinking holes for the ranch's small herd of cattle. The slopes were sage-covered, the hilltops a combination of scrub and occasional stands of aspen. Unlike the completely forested knobs at home, the vistas were immense. The mountain peaks in the distance were rocky and patched with snow. A blue sky stretched from one horizon to the other.

Terry, full of information about the wildflowers, occasionally stopped to snap photos for the field guide she was writing. One day, Gerry led me to an aspen stand and courteously indulged my request to photograph Dancer and me slipping among the trees' white with black, paint-like slashed bark, à la characters in a Bev Doolittle camouflage painting. (Google a photo of her *Woodland Encounter*.)

From a painter's model, I morphed into a movie starlet on Bonanza. Instead of Dancer, I was riding Cochise, Little Joe Cartwright's black-and-white Paint, on the Ponderosa. The little girl from the big Midwestern city, watching television Westerns in her cowgirl outfit, was finally living her dream. I was out West, riding the range!

June-July, 2013

CHAPTER 34
SHADOW SELVES

The late afternoon shadows we cast across the trails this fall fascinated me. As Highlander and I walked through the forest, they followed us companionably one moment, suddenly abandoned us the next, like a pet dog temporarily chasing after invisible prey only to return when the inclination hit. I tried to freeze and preserve some of these ephemeral, elusive images with the camera on my cell phone.

It wasn't easy to remove my gloves, twist my fanny pack to a tummy pack, unzip it, fish out the phone, and switch on the camera prior to arriving at a spot where the sun was spilling out of the woods and onto the trail. Nor was snapping complete and focused shots from a moving horse. Fortunately, Highlander usually lets me ride reinless when I'm in photography mode—only once did I have to stuff my phone in my mouth and grab the reins off his neck to redirect him. Unfortunately, however, I had to delete most of the photos due to missing body parts, poor focus, and bad lighting.

During this season of artistic experimentation, I attended a weekly book discussion led by Reverend Ray at church. Daily reflection was the foundation of Robert Brumet's *Living Originally: Ten Spiritual Practices to Transform Your Life*. I was already struggling to find enough time and energy to do all my chores, work two part-time jobs, oversee a kitchen renovation, meet with my writing group, start a grant application, and ride Highlander—let alone

79

to read the book, attend the book discussions, and meditate daily. I did my best and tried not to beat myself up when I fell short.

During the last discussion, I had two *aha!* moments. One, by riding alone, I could kill two birds with one stone: exercising my "easy keeper," who gains weight all too easily, and meditating. Home meditation doesn't work for me. I get distracted by the ceiling cobweb that needs removal, the blinds and furniture that need dusting, the windows and dishes that need washing, the cat and dog bowls that need refilling, the pet hair that needs vacuuming, the books that need straightening, etc., etc., etc. When I ride with others, we talk. Riding "alone" in the woods is as holy, if not holier, than attending church (in my humble opinion).

Two, the shadow self was a concept described in the book. Basically, it's the part of us hidden from our conscious awareness. Dark shadows mask our true selves and cause us pain. They are gifts in disguise, trying to reveal our inner aspects that need healing. By exposing them to the light of our awareness, we can dissipate them and more fully become who we were created to be and thus shine more brightly in the world.

With these thoughts in mind, I publicly committed to riding Highlander solo during the next three days prior to firearm deer season—perhaps we could hunt up a shadow or two that needed confronting. My choice to ride that very afternoon was rewarded with lighting perfect for the creation of shadows. Mesmerized, I added more snapshots to my collection.

* * *

I loved how Highlander and I, serving as sundials, saw our shadows change with the time of day. Always opposite the sun, they are longest in the morning and evening and shortest at midday, when the sun is at its highest. Just as our physical position relative to the sun determines the size of our physical shadows, it is when our spirits most closely align with God on High that our dark shadows retreat.

November, 2013

CHAPTER 35
IN CLOUD NINE

Highlander, remember when we first met? You were a tub of baby fat just starting out under saddle. Despite your plodding slowness, I didn't think I was experienced enough to ride an untrained horse and temporarily passed that honor on to a younger woman. The year 2000 found us competing in our first (25-mile) endurance ride together. How I love the "On Cloud Nine" photo of us taken during it—your hooves lost in the cloud of dust you kicked up, your tack a rainbow of borrowed, mismatched pieces, and me grinning broadly. Then, two years later, Jim and I bought you for my 50th birthday.

Early August had been unusually wet, so one day, during a break in the weather, I decided to sneak in a trail ride on Highlander. Despite my dwindling energy and the overcast sky, I put off some chores and quickly drove to the stable to tack him up.

We headed into the forest around 6:30 pm. The comfortable temperature, dearth of biting insects, and threat of rain revitalized our youthful daring. Fortunately, I had retained enough maturity, however, to securely tie my poncho behind my saddle in the event of a sudden downpour.

After meandering through the woods from the valley up to a favorite ridge trail we hadn't trod in a while, we turned left.

The trail had slimmed down from its old fire road girth; soft, ground-in earth now topped most of the gravel that had been laid down years ago. The sandstone grains were moist but not muddy and matched Highlander's chestnut mane and coat. The gauntlet of overhanging branches sprinkled us continuously with water collected from the morning's storm. We were alone, just him and me, perfect company in our private world. The vegetative green accenting Highlander's red coat began to dim. Birdsong transitioned to insect song—the towhee's "drink your tea" to cricket chirp. By the time we got to the end of the trail and turned around, it was twilight. We gaily ran back along the ridge and started our darkening descent to the lake in the valley. I have good night vision, but, as hard as I tried, I couldn't see anything clearly. I squinted, slid my glasses down my nose, rubbed my nearsighted eyes, and still, nothing focused. I was about to fling off my glasses in frustration when I realized that we were travelling through the condensation of a humungous cloud!

Like a ghost, it was invisible, yet it obscured everything it contained and was felt more than seen. I emotionally felt my entry into and exit out of the cloud. It's hard to put into words. Imagine the surprise of a helium balloon or a kite being slowly and gloriously released on its long tether to dance in the air, then being unexpectedly and slowly pulled back to earth. Or, picture yourself at the base of a dive, being released by the water's pressure and slowly floating back to the surface. It's a brief, rare, out-of-your-element voyage followed by a gentle reentry into familiar normalcy.

It was still twilight when Highlander and I emerged from the cloud. The twilight soon merged undetectably into dusk, and the dusk imperceptibly transitioned into darkness. Three happy hours after departure, we could see the barn's pole light in the distance, and then, as we drew closer, the flashlight beam of the barn manager coming out to see if we were okay. Okay? Highlander was ready to get naked, roll in the pasture, and eat supper, and I was in seventh heaven! A spell had been cast—I felt more tranquil and more deeply relaxed than I had in a very long time.

Highlander, I should rename you Magic!

August, 2014. A variation of this tale—named "XX and OO"—was published by Per Bastet Publications in XX: SIW Goes Platinum by the Southern Indiana Writers in 2016.

CHAPTER 36
HAPPY TRAILS, LINDA

I met Linda one Saturday in the parking lot of an elementary school serving as a county recycling center. She drove up in a truck pulling a trailer loaded with two horses. She and her passenger were going riding as soon as she deposited her recyclables—which took a while because several people wanted to meet her horses.

Linda and I became riding buddies and fast friends. For her 66th birthday, two years later, I made her a necklace because she was a strong supporter of my horsehair jewelry business. Shockingly, she suddenly and unexpectedly passed away on Thursday, January 16, 2014, at the age of 68. I am still reeling from her loss. I don't have a picture of her eight-string necklace to show you, but here is its story.

When I offered to make Linda a bracelet from the hair of her beloved seven horses and one pony, she requested a necklace with magnetic clasps due to her arthritis. Because the hair she provided was only long enough for a choker and I had not yet mastered braiding on additional hair, I created two chokers which she could fasten together into a long necklace or wear as wrap-around wrist and ankle bracelets. Linda told me that she loved her jewelry, but I never realized how much until I attended her funeral home visitation on Sunday.

Her reception line started in the hall. Her room was packed with pink and purple flowers, memorabilia spanning her life, and people of all ages. It took Jim and me 45 minutes to reach Linda and her family. As we drew near, we passed bales of hay bearing a bridle full of "bling" and two saddles, one a silver-plated parade model. Standing at the foot of Linda's casket was one of her sons. I presented a print of a photo of Linda that I had snapped with my cell phone during our last ride together and had captioned "Happy Trails." He smiled, thanked me, and placed it on a saddle.

Adorning the closed end of Linda's casket was a blanket of pink roses her husband of 35 years had selected. I barely recognized Linda's torso in the open end. She was still instead of in constant motion, quiet instead of talking, and wearing a dress instead of jeans. Her hair was styled instead of in pony tails. Among the items in the pulled-out drawer above her abdomen was her long horsehair necklace.

When I returned to the funeral home the next morning, I noticed that the necklace had migrated onto her pillow. Before we non-family members were excused for the private casket closing, her husband okayed my spontaneous request for a fellow attendee to call my cell phone so everyone, especially Linda, could hear its ring tone. Human conversation ceased when horses whinnied and lip-sputtered and didn't pick up again until someone amened, "Happy Trails!"

Linda's parade to the church was very long. During her packed funeral Mass, the priest duly noted Linda's love of horses, in addition to her love of family, friends, dogs, and cats. They, he said, were God's gifts to her, and her devotion to them was her gift to God. Dale Evans and Roy Rogers sang Linda out of church via a tape of "Happy Trails to You."

Two horses greeted her hearse at the cemetery. The riderless palomino was wearing Linda's parade saddle, "blingy" bridle, and blanket of roses. Mounted on its black companion was a longtime friend of Linda's, dressed in black. A pallbearer quietly rolled Linda over to the horses for a silent equine blessing.

How incomprehensible it was for this big-hearted woman, who had never met a stranger, to die at a hospital during an outpatient exam, yet how merciful it was that she lived life fully up to a quick end. I sorely miss riding with Linda and talking to her on the trail and on the phone about all things "horse." Happy trails, my good friend!

January, 2014

CHAPTER 37
MANIFESTATIONS REALIZED IN ALBERTA, CANADA

During the summer of 2014, I received an Individual Artist Program grant from the Indiana Arts Commission to help finance a trip to Alberta, Canada to study under Donna, a master horsehair artist. On my one day off (on my own dime) I enjoyed a glorious 5-hour trail ride—on a cool, July morning with low humidity and blue sky—at Waterton National Park, north of Montana's Glacier National Park.

The almost-private highway south out of Lethbridge, a gray strip bisecting plains awash in yellow canola flowers and green grass stretching to the horizon on both sides. Round rolls of hay resembling giant biscuits of shredded wheat cereal, small and large square bales—the large ones randomly scattered or stacked into stooks (pyramids of ten). Occasional rows of sleek, white windmills.

* * *

Eventually, a suggestion of something ahead in the distance, or, then again, maybe not. A mirage? No, the slow solidification of vapor into a mountain range!

* * *

At my destination, Waterton National Park, a five-hour ride on a mare named Blue—a sturdy, surefooted blue roan Quarter

Horse who wanted to graze, but wasn't supposed to as she carried me through nature's magnificent salad bar. (Although sporting a Western saddle, she responded better to English reining—one rein per hand, each slightly played with a finger—than to neck reining, both reins in one hand.)

A slow climb partially through a riotous mix of tall, multi-colored wildflowers of various species—(a traverse through a giant, living bouquet!)

A lonely bear cub crossing the trail in front of us, (please, may there be no overprotective mamma as we pass!)

Clomping across an impressively well-built bridge above a clear stream roaring swiftly down a jumble of broken mountain rock.

Lunch halfway down at a lake rimmed by peaks. (The trail guide cut two apples from my hotel's breakfast bar; he, I, and the two women from Calgary accompanying us, fed the halves to our horses.)

A tipi campground in the valley at the bottom (where were the Native Americans?) and two more crossings through the stream—much wider and a little slower now, but still splashing through a bed of large-grade rocks.

(Pull up your legs or you'll get wet to your knees! And don't look down or you might get dizzy and fall off your horse!)

Then, much too soon, after a short rise, full circle back to the stable.

* * *

Like the formation of the Rockies from the mist, my trip to Canada to study with an inspirational artist—including this one day off for sight-seeing, as well as the creation of my braided horsehair jewelry business—had manifested from the energy contained in the conception of an idea, testimony to Napoleon Hill's *"What the mind can conceive and believe, it can receive"* and the Unity Church's *"Thoughts held in mind, produce after their kind."*

Thank you, God, for this tremendous gift!

July, 2014

CHAPTER 38
ENLIGHTENMENT

usings to my horse. . .

M   If humans are superior to animals, then why were you seemingly born with spiritual qualities that I have yet to master? Despite all my religious schooling, church-going, praying, inspirational reading, and striving, I still struggle to quiet my busy, anxious mind and live in the moment.

I wish I could attain your full immersion and engagement in the present and eliminate my persistent judgment and resistance, my regret and reliving of the past, and my fretting over and planning of the future.

I wish I could better accept what life presents me, better maintain my equilibrium, live more simply, and achieve your typical slow, full, rhythmic, yogic, and restful breathing. There is so much we humans can learn from you "lesser" animals. You, my dear horse, are a guru!

September, 2014

89

CHAPTER 39
MY KIND OF MUSIC—
A RANT ABOUT NOISE

I prefer quiet to noise—including recorded music which is so often imposed, played repetitively, and accompanied by inane commercials and DJ chatter, all of which distract me from my own thoughts and feelings and make me yearn to jump on my horse and run for the woods.

Call me old-fashioned, but I don't watch music videos. And I prefer the book version of a story to the movie one because I favor my own imagination and interpretation over someone else's.

Civilization is just too darn noisy. I can't read in a waiting room anymore because of a TV (nay, TVs) blaring—the channel usually selected by a stranger with completely different taste. I have to strain to carry on a conversation in a restaurant (not exactly conducive to digestion) because of the stereo blaring and multiple flashing TVs tuned to different channels. Most times, after driving considerable mileage to visit people, I struggle to catch up with them because of the TV on in the room.

Speaking about TV, why are huge TV screens and home theaters so fashionable now, when the quality of most programming has nosedived? So many shows are un-educational and uninspiring, so violent and vulgar. And the news is downright upsetting.

Don't get me started on cell phones and social (often antisocial) media, another form of failed potential. In days of yore,

90

people in public excused themselves and retreated to phone booths to talk in private. Today, many think nothing of sharing private, even intimate matters in public. TMI for me!

I guess we humans haven't evolved enough to use the various forms of technological communication exclusively for good. Their lure, combined with the addictiveness of instant gratification, has contributed to the decay of good manners in our society, or so I believe. Sounding off with one's opinion without first getting the facts seems in vogue (despite that being so much easier and faster now, due to search engines). Gone are the days of hand-writing our gut reaction on paper, sleeping on the matter, tearing up our first response, and rewriting a polite, constructive edition the next day. Why are rudeness and cussing now trumping manners? Education and self-control used to connote strength; today, bullying, name-calling, ignorance, and violence are all too common.

Why are we in such desperate need of constant distraction and diversion? Why are we so disconnected from our inner selves? Why are we so averse to quiet and being alone? What are we afraid of?

Shouldn't we spend more time listening than talking, learning than pontificating, controlling our emotions and framing our words before speaking, discussing ideas instead of ranting monologs, inspiring rather than degrading, unifying instead of dividing, solving problems instead of creating them, taking responsibility instead of blaming, and researching facts rather than blindly reacting to fiction? And what about contemplation and prayer? Wouldn't the world be a better place if we talked more with God and less to each other?

Personally, nature is my kind of music, and rides on Highlander through the woods are my videos. The score that accompanied today's ride was an entire symphony—the clip-clop of his hooves striking different surfaces, the wind whipping past my ears during our gallops, the squeak of my leather saddle, the jingle of the hardware on his bridle, the chirping of insects and birds in the background—sights and sounds that calm and settle and soothe and inspire me.

Story's insertion-point guesstimated

CHAPTER 40
JETTISON!

"To bring the sublime into the mundane is the greatest challenge there is,"

Pir Vilayat Inayat Khan, Sufi Master

Highlander splatted manure onto the concrete cross-tie pad as we tacked up outside the barn. After I removed the pile and swung into the saddle, we headed west down the lane past the pastures.

Once in the woods, Highlander veered off and paused. Translation: "I have to urinate and would prefer to do so at a halt and with a semblance of privacy." When I signaled "okay" by removing all my leg pressure from his sides, he carefully stepped his front legs forward, stiffened them, and slowly stretched out his body. As he watered the undergrowth, I stood in my stirrups to release some weight from his kidneys.

His business finished, Highlander stepped back onto the lane and followed it the short distance to its T with a gravel fire road on state property. A short way in, Highlander plopped down more manure as if to mark our entry point.

The fall color peak was over—no multi-colored leaves rained to the ground like confetti. Instead, curled, drying leaves masked the gravel. They, and the falling leaves netted by the pine saplings, had overbaked to a narrow spectrum of brown into which he, a dark chestnut, was almost absorbed. To prevent a hunter from mistaking Highlander for a deer, I'd Velcroed orange strips of fleece around the brow band and cheek straps of his halter-bridle.

We turned onto the dirt single track, and Highlander volleyed more manure balls into the leaf litter that was all but obscuring the trail.

By then the frequency of Highlander's "nature calls" had reached alarm status in my consciousness. Was it normal? Was something wrong with him? How serious was it? Did I need to call the vet? However does one treat such a malady?

I calmed down. My thoughts shifted. Perhaps Highlander was pranking me—pretending he didn't know the trails and needed to mark our way back to the barn with the only material available to him. Or maybe he was determined to tell me something important, and, because I hadn't yet gotten his message, he was repeating it and would keep repeating it until I did. Finally, I figured it out!

Having grown up on the trails on this state property, my companion knew what lay in store for us next—three short-but-steep roller coaster hills to the ridge. At 21½ and past his prime, he could no longer run the whole ascent. So, perhaps like 72-year old Mr. Potato Richardson, who'd won his third demanding 100-mile Tevis Cup endurance race in the Sierra Nevadas earlier this year, Highlander knew it was time to adopt a "ride smarter" strategy more befitting maturity.

Highlander had simply been jettisoning weight to avoid packing it up the challenging climb ahead! (Better his waste than my body! My heavy saddle and I were already enough of a handicap—one, thank goodness, he was still gallantly willing to carry.)

Moreover, perhaps my trusty steed was modeling what I need to do more often—jettison emotional and mental baggage so as to more easily proceed along the trail of life, and, in the process, allow my less-burdened soul to soar a little higher!

November, 2015

CHAPTER 41
HIDDEN TREASURES

I found a geode in Highlander's pasture today. I can't wait to ask the barn manager, a jack-of-all-trades, to crack it open for me. I love the revelation of crystals magically growing inside a cave ball small enough to hold in my hand.

We humans are geodes, our bodies aged and worn on the outside, our spirits still shiny and forming on the inside. Our core is the still, quiet space where God dwells. I've heard it said that we, too, must be cracked open—not only to let light in but also to let our inner light shine out and express God in the world.

Today, as Highlander and I rode, we weren't merely walking the hour-long, amorphous trail through the woods around the barn and pastures, we were tracing the shape of a geode! Inside its outline, a thick band of trees rimmed a large, grassy core. From the moment Highlander and I left the barn to the moment we returned, he and his left-behind, out-of-sight, pasture buddies, each a treasure to someone, whinnied back and forth. I've never heard such a long equine conversation! Had the horses been discussing how to get the slice-of-geode image through my hard head and into my brain? Oh, how I wish I could speak Horse!

OMG. . . I owe my very writing voice to horses!

And, now that I am gathering my horse tales for publication, I wonder if I am willing to crack myself open wide enough to let those strangers in.

* * *

Post Script: When I shared this quandary with my writers' club, a poet challenged me to instead anticipate the admittance of new friends.

March, 2016

CHAPTER 42
FURTHER MEDITATION

To let light in or to let light out?

In *Paracelsus I*, Robert Browning says it's to let light out:

Truth is within ourselves; it takes no rise
From outward things, whate'er you may believe.
There is an inmost centre in us all,
Where truth abides in fullness; and around,
Wall upon wall, the gross flesh hems it in,
This perfect, clear perception—which is truth.
A baffling and perverting carnal mesh
Binds it and makes all error: and, to KNOW,
Rather consists in opening out a way
Whence the imprisoned splendor may escape,
Than in effecting entry for a light.

But *Unity* says to let light in:

". . .I prioritize my spiritual growth by devoting time and energy to God. Spiritual texts and other resources help me to learn and deepen my understanding of faith-based teachings.

I bring what I have learned into my life through my thoughts, words, and actions. I create daily practices that support my further seeking of God.

96

As I grow and allow more of God's light into my life, my true self is further revealed."

(The Daily Word's 1/31/2017 meditation on 'unfolding'). Reprinted with permission of Unity®, publisher of Daily Word®.)

* * *

Perhaps a crack is really supposed to do both—let light flow both out and in.

Note: Emphasis in both quotes are mine.

February, 2017

CHAPTER 43
BLACKBERRIES AND BLACK BEARS

I was at the barn and didn't give a hoot about the thunder booming in the distance nor the start of the rain. I hadn't ridden in over a week—mainly due to the hot, humid weather and the black bear sighting—and was determined to get out on Highlander. As long as there was no lightning.

According to Indiana's DNR website, black bears abundantly roamed the state, except for the northwest prairie region, until 1850, when their population plummeted due to habitat loss and unregulated hunting. There were no confirmed black bear sightings from 1871 until June of 2015, when a young male wandered in from the north. Shortly after emerging from hibernation in April, he was trapped and killed, reportedly because he'd lost his fear of humans. Earlier this July, a male from Kentucky crossed the Ohio River into Southern Indiana. Just one week ago, on the 23rd, pictures of him at the lake near Highlander's stable were posted on the Internet.

This morning, a friend Facebooked that horse flies were out in record numbers around the lake. So I doused Highlander with a spray made from natural ingredients that I'm experimenting with, replaced his heavier pasture face mask with his lighter riding mask, and attached his mesh rump rug—its front ties to the back of my saddle, and its back ties around the dock of his tail. To keep myself and my saddle dry, I donned my long yellow saddle slicker.

Once off stable property, Highlander and I turned onto a logging road in the process of getting a new base coat of coarse-grade
gravel. As we tripped through it, I was glad that Highlander had
just gotten all four of his shoes reset. When we rounded a bend
and saw a small bulldozer parked ahead next to a pile of finer-grade
gravel for top coating, Highlander went into full drama-king
mode. For a good while, he enjoyed backing up and spinning
around under the pretense of being too terrified to approach it.
This from a horse who had passed the bulldozer several times and
hadn't even flinched when, recently, a logging truck had all but
pinned us against a fence while passing us on a blacktop road.

The gravel ended at a stream crossing just beyond the dozer.
Highlander sloshed through the water and slopped up a muddy
hill. The trail solidified at the top, the dirt so quiet that we realized that the thunder and rain had quit. The silence was truly
deafening.

It's funny how yins and yangs—like wet and dry, noise and
quiet—help you appreciate opposites. My stomach started growl-
ing. We were on the ridge, halfway through our ride, but I still
hadn't seen a solo, let alone a pint of the juicy blackberries I was
looking forward to feasting upon. It's a good thing I had stuffed an
apple for Highlander and a nut bar for myself in my fanny pack.

It turned out we weren't the only ones hungry. Highlander
and I were almost carried away by a swarm—nay, a flock—of
dive-bombing, female horse flies focused on slitting open our
skin and lapping up our blood to obtain the protein necessary
to produce eggs.

On our way back down to the valley, we saw lots of butterflies
greedily guzzling "manure juice" from the fresh horse droppings
on the trail, and nectar from the mauve thistle flowers starting to
bloom alongside. Orange-brown fritillaries freckled with black
markings and some Eastern Tiger Swallowtails were companionably sharing their sweet treat with some bees. The male "tigers"
are yellow with black stripes and a few orange and blue spots
near their tails. The females come in two color phases: yellow
with black stripes and more blue spots than the male; and black

with even more blue spots. Blue is my favorite color, and I so love the dusky shade of the dots.

Small, white doilies of Queen Anne's lace were also abloom. My former students, who found plants less interesting than animals, had liked this "scratch and sniff" plant because they could dig up its roots and release its carrot odor, the reason it also goes by the name Wild Carrot.

Their favorite flower, jewelweed, was starting to bloom in the valley. Kids love this "action" plant. They can pluck off a leaf and magically silver plate it by immersing it into a stream or a glass of water. (Repelled by the leaf's oily coating, the surrounding water turns into tiny bubbles). Even better, when the orange, horn-shaped flowers are replaced by small, zucchini-looking fruits in early fall, kids can, by touching a ripe end, trigger the fruit to self-peel (picture a mini-banana) thereby spitting out a volley of small seeds in all directions for an impressive distance.

When Highlander and I emerged from the woods, we came up behind a wild turkey trotting ahead of us alongside his pasture. Right before it got to the barn, it slipped under the fence, turned right, and passed through the pasture to the woods on the other side.

The black bear? Fortunately, or unfortunately—I can't quite decide which—we never saw him. Some folks thought he'd headed back south to Kentucky. If I were him? I'd head north in pursuit of a fresh blackberry crop!

July, 2016

PART II

EARLY ADULTHOOD

CHAPTER 44
GERONIMO!

*S*o how did I get here? Part II of my memoir is mostly about my first horse, an Appaloosa gelding, named Geronimo. This section of my memoir takes place in my 20s, after I'd earned my B.S. and started teaching.

Geronimo was a pacer with the habit of running his riders into trees. Fortunately, Ulla, the Danish manager/riding and instructor/trainer at his barn, kept a very strict eye on both of us. She taught me how to care for a horse, taught Geronimo how to trot, and helped me develop my balance and feel. Many of our dressage lessons included lots of lunging and cavaletti work. Eventually, Geronimo and I graduated from the ring to safe, harmonious, solo trail rides. Mange tak, laerer! (Danish for "Thank you, teacher!")

Geronimo and Me, 1976

CHAPTER 45
A WINTER RIDE

At midafternoon, it was clear and barely above zero. Six inches of snow blanketed the ground. Upon fetching Geronimo from the pasture, I laughed as he so carefully stepped *over* a snowdrift as if it were a solid obstacle.

After tacking up in the barn, we departed for a long ride. The first part, through the adjoining field, was familiar yet interesting. (I really enjoy watching the field's appearance change with the seasons.) Soon, we came upon three sleds and four shrieking kids—Geronimo bravely passed them all by! Then he waded through a cold, surprisingly still-flowing stream and entered a narrow path into the woods.

White snow, inches thick, covered barely-visible brown limbs and trunks. Above, through the branches, I could glimpse portions of the clear blue sky. It was so quiet (the fresh snow completely muffled the sound of Geronimo's hooves) and beautiful that, for the moment, I felt sheltered in a fairyland.

We emerged onto a path bordering an expansive field. The sunlit goldenrod and Queen Anne's lace matched the rich hue of Geronimo's rust Appaloosa markings. The snow matched his white markings. The only other color apparent was the blue of his eyes and the now completely-visible sky.

It wasn't so protected there in the field. In fact, a constant, cold wind made me lose feeling in my ears, nose, and face. I ached with cold until a half-mile trot warmed me up a bit. We circled around by another trail bowered with snow-laden trees so beautiful I had to shout. Our spell of privacy was broken when we crossed back over the stream and headed to the barn. What an incredible ride!

1975

CHAPTER 46
A FALL RIDE

Two frisky horses
Late October, leaves half gone
Two laughing riders
Galloping along the creek
Four creatures celebrating life

1977

CHAPTER 47
DREAMS

My fourth-year teaching assignment was high school biology. A composition class was added soon after the school year began. Eager to teach my two favorite subjects but never having taught composition before, I continued the format of the previous teacher—something along the lines of spelling on Monday, grammar on Tuesday, capitalization on Wednesday, punctuation on Thursday, and writing on Friday. I loved Fridays most of all. At the beginning of class, I handed each student a copy of the completed piece I had started the previous week—and they handed me theirs. Then, in silence until the bell rang, we began new compositions.

During weekends, I enjoyed learning about my students' lives and interests as I edited their work. *"Dreams"* is one of the tales I wrote for them.

* * *

Dreams Really do Come True!
Ever since I can remember, I have been interested in horses. As a little girl, I was an avid fan of television Westerns (Bonanza, The Lone Ranger, Wagon Trail, The Rifleman, etc.) and series which starred horses (Fury, My Friend Flicka, Mr. Ed, National Velvet, etc.). I devoured every horse book in the public library.

In grade school, my best friend and I collected horse statues and clipped horse pictures from newspapers and magazines.

Occasionally, my Camp Fire group rented stable horses for hour-long rides in the park. Twice—once at summer camp and once as a CYO member—I took a series of riding lessons. One summer after getting my driver's license, I even leased a horse.

But it wasn't until I received my first teaching job that I had the opportunity to become seriously involved with horses. In exchange for the evening care of an Appaloosa gelding named Geronimo, I received riding privileges. When Geronimo was put up for sale, I bought him. I took dressage lessons for two years. Then Geronimo and I began trail riding in addition to our ring work.

Recently, a school librarian, a member of the Ohio Horsemen's Council, invited me to her organization's annual Memorial Weekend Trail Ride at Indiana's Brown County State Park.

Last Thursday, she trailered Geronimo to her farm. On Friday, we hitched her camper to her pick-up. Three-and-a-half hours later, we arrived at the Horse Campground. We unloaded Sully and Geronimo and took them on a short ride to stretch their legs. Afterward, we tied them to the hitching post next to our rig and hayed, watered, and grained them. Then I got introduced to her friends.

On Saturday, our party of eleven went on a 30-mile trail ride. Besides Geronimo, there were other Appaloosas as well as Arabs, American Saddlebreds, and Quarter Horses. They included other geldings as well as mares and a stallion. We rode up ridges, through hollows, and along a river valley. Eight hot, dusty hours later, we returned to camp, exhausted.

On Sunday, six of us rode through the woods to Crooked Creek Lake and back. We covered twenty-six miles in seven hours. Monday, we stayed closer to camp and completed a twelve-mile circuit in three hours.

Except for it being too short, the weekend was terrific! The 300 square miles of Brown County State Park resembled the Smokies. The woods were beautiful—full of blooming wildflowers and singing warblers. The weather was clear and sunny. The people I was with couldn't have been nicer. And Geronimo was so good—I was very pleased with him.

I had wanted a horse of my own for so long—and three years ago, I bought one. I had wanted to go on a horseback riding and camping trip for years—and last weekend, I did. Don't ever give up your dreams—work to make them come true. Your life will be all the richer for doing so.

1978

CHAPTER 48
TOUCHED BY AN ARCHANGEL

The Man: I spent the summer after my fifth year of teaching in Northeast Ohio, helping my family build a new home. To maintain a connection to horses, I took riding lessons at a stable in a city park. My teacher was Michael von der Nonne, a dressage instructor in his early 80s who had recently, after surgery, graduated from a wheel chair to a cane. Somehow, he charmed me—who had zero interest in competing—into preparing for a training-level dressage competition.

After lessons on the school horse (Hungarian Dancer!) he'd selected for me, I sometimes drove Michael home. He lived on the second floor of an old-style, two-story, multiplex with a wooden deck extending across the back. Michael would invite me in, and I would accept, not only to enjoy his company but also to be sure he made it up the steps and into his apartment safely. He had been born in Russia, and I was fascinated by the foreign cigar smell and the Russian Orthodox icons decorating his walls. He served me interesting new foods—such as borscht soup and European-style bread you broke apart instead of slicing—as we talked about horses. It was so wonderful to finally have a hometown friend who shared my passion.

As the competition neared, Michael schooled me in the required uniform—breeches and a blouse with a stand-up collar and horse pin. He took me to the stable's consignment shop for a helmet and a pair of English riding boots. The only pair that fit my feet didn't extend high enough up my long, skinny calves. Michael recommended hiring a shoe repairman to add extensions and polish the new and old leathers to disguise the seams in between. He showed me what style of jacket I needed and suggested that I purchase a pattern and material so a seamstress could sew one with sleeves long enough to reach my wrists. I felt so sophisticated, yet odd, in my new outfit—even a bit racy, as the black jacket had a shiny red lining.

Dressage riders and their horses compete by riding increasingly difficult, required patterns in an arena, one horse and rider at a time. Our score wasn't high, but we completed the introductory pattern I was so worried about forgetting.

After the competition, I returned to the southwestern part of the state for the new school year. Then I sold Geronimo and moved out of state to a large university, where I missed the company of horses and horse people.

Thus, in 1981, after a visit to my family, I decided to pop in on Michael on my way back to school. I climbed his back steps, walked down the porch to his door, and knocked. Not hearing any sound from within his apartment, I called his name. A next-door neighbor came out and very gently said, "Honey, he doesn't live here anymore." As I was about to ask where he moved, she added, "He passed away." In shock and tears, I could only get two words out: "How?" and "When?"

I cried when Michael's neighbor told me when and how he'd died—while crossing the street to shop at a convenience store, he was struck and killed by a hit-and-run driver.

After answering my questions, she slipped inside and brought out a photocopy of Michael's biography, *Historian's Column, U.S. Dressage Federation, November, 1980.*

I later found a detailed account of a special event mentioned in it, *Lipizzan Team Wins a Great Race, by Dr. Delphi Toth, Lipizzan Association of North America's Haute Ecole, Vol. 17, Issue 2, 2008.*

Below is my synopsis of a combination of the two.

The Legend: *Michael was born in 1897 in St. Petersburg. His Prussian (German) grandfather had become a Russian citizen after accompanying Princess Charlotte there for her marriage to the future Czar (Nicholas I), and was by then a retired general. Michael's father and an uncle supplied Michael with a steady string of mounts as he grew up—a donkey, a small mountain horse, a half-Arabian, and retired military chargers. Michael entered a military cavalry academy in 1913, graduated in 1915, and served as second lieutenant in a cavalry regiment until 1917.*

After the Bolshevik (Communist) Revolution in October, soldiers killed thousands of officers, claiming they were 'enemies of the people.' To save their lives, Michael and some other officers removed their uniforms, stopped shaving, journeyed south by night for 10 days in a small wagon pulled by draft horses, and joined the Volunteer White Army. In late 1920, the army was evacuated to Turkey by British and French Allies. Two years later, several countries offered the troops asylum. Michael chose the Kingdom of Serbs, Croats, and Slovenes (Yugoslavia). He became assistant trainer at a racetrack, then manager of a Lipizzan breeding farm. In 1925, he was promoted to a stallion station where he managed 50 Lipizzans, 15 Arabs, and 15 Thoroughbreds and started a school with a two-year training program for grooms and riders. There, he got to exercise several veteran horses from the Spanish Riding Court in Vienna. During September, 1927, Michael competed in a 255-km (158½ -mile) endurance ride designed to test the ability of the three different breeds. He captained the Lipizzan team, comprised of four mares that he and three of his 15-year-old students rode. The competition was a team of half-Arab stallions, a team of pure-bred Arabian stallions, and a mixed team of full- and half-blooded Thoroughbred stallions.

A purebred Arabian was the first horse and the only one from its team to complete—in 24 hours and 23 minutes. Michael's team of "Lipizzan Ladies," the only team to complete, rode in together at 25 hours and 17 minutes. Three half-Arabian stallions and one Thoroughbred stallion completed many hours later. Michael's team was declared the winner, and he received 15,000 dinars, enough to retire from his state job and move to Belgrade, where he leased a stable and started his own riding center to better support his wife and two children. During the German invasion of Yugoslavia in 1941, the Yugoslav army mobilized Michael's horses, his diplomatic clients left the country, and the Germans heavily bombed the city. Michael and his family moved to German-annexed Austria where his son attended the university. Michael worked with his wife and daughter in an apiary until he was drafted into the German Wehrmacht and placed in command of a horse-drawn transportation unit.

Upon its demobilization by the American Army at the end of WWII, Michael moved to Munich to look for his family. At that time, the city was the location of the U.S. Army Olympic Team. In addition to the horses the team had brought from the U.S., it had inherited 40 top German horses from the war. Michael and two other officers were hired to exercise and train all the horses until 1948, when the team left for the Olympic Games in London. Michael remained as a riding instructor at Maximilian University until he and his family immigrated to the U.S. in 1953. After working two years on the New York Central Railroad, he found full-time employment as a horse trainer and riding instructor in Northeast Ohio.

During the late 1970s, Michael spent several years in a wheelchair due to severe arthritis in his hip joints. After bravely risking their replacement with synthetic ones, he was able to sit a horse again and enjoy pleasure riding in his early 80s.

* * *

Broadway

Thirty-two years after my attempted visit to Michael, I was powerfully reminded of him. My husband had treated me to a visiting performance of War Horse, the Broadway play set during WWI and starring life-size horse puppets. During it, I wondered if anyone else in the audience had known a real WWI cavalry soldier and what Michael would have thought about the play or the 1982 children's novel it was based upon.

What were the odds that Michael and I, born on different continents during different generations, his at the end of one century and mine in the middle of the next, would meet? His early life was totally dependent upon the horse, and my whole life was after the role of horses had shrunk to sports and recreation. His life was epic, and mine was ordinary. What an honor the nobleman, soldier, and gentleman who'd taught Olympic riders and the wealthy, had bestowed upon me by totally "getting" and nurturing my mysterious horse fever!

I think of Michael more often now that I'm fighting the stiffening of my own joints by taking Pilates. I want to ride well into my 80s!

* * *

Post Script: Interestingly, Michael and Joseph Pilates were contemporaries whose lives shared some commonalities: Joseph was born in Germany, developed his exercise form while interred in Britain during WWI, later immigrated to the U.S., and taught his passion at the New York City Ballet.

1979, 1981, and 2013

CHAPTER 49
MY WORST NIGHTMARE

After six years of teaching (in various public schools and one parochial one), and wrangling with the decision, I decided to pursue a master's degree. I wanted to get into a better-paying profession that would allow me to delve deeper into the horse world. The problems were that to attend the university of my choice, I had to take out a student loan and sell Geronimo.

One day, a man responded to my Horse for Sale ad and made an appointment to meet me at the stable. I arrived early to groom and saddle Geronimo. When the perspective buyer arrived, I lunged Geronimo clockwise and counterclockwise at the walk and trot and then mounted to repeat the process. I explained my reason for having to sell Geronimo, his breeding, age, and history, and stated my asking price. The man was clean-cut, polite, well-spoken, seemed interested, and said he'd get back to me.

As soon as he left, the stable owner barreled over. "Do you know who that was?" she asked. When I said no, she said, "He's a killer." Worried that I had unknowingly invited a criminal onto her property, I wondered who and how many people the killer had done away with, how he'd done the deeds, and why he was loose. Was he an escaped convict on the run, or had he reformed after serving his sentence? Then she explained what a kill buyer is: a person who turns a profit by buying and reselling horses, the fatter the better, to the "glue factory."

I was shocked. Geronimo wasn't old, ill, or fatally injured. That was when the tough old cowboy on television had teared up and mercifully shot his best friend, who had saved his life several times over, with a quick bullet to the head. Or the Native American brave who thanked the Great Spirit for his horse's service during life, and then, after shooting an arrow into its heart, had prayed a thank-you for the horse's body, the parts of which would help sustain his village. I thought all people had relationships with their horses. It was chilling to learn that there were those who had dollar signs in their eyes and regarded these sentient beings as mere commodities.

Selling Geronimo to anyone was already hard enough, but knowing that not everyone who shows an interest in horses is motivated by love made it even more difficult. Thankfully, the man never contacted me again. I was careful to inquire about the intentions of future prospective buyers and ended up selling Geronimo to a family who wanted a riding horse.

I don't know why, but I didn't keep in touch with them after I moved away. For a while, my old roommate reported seeing Geronimo as she drove past his new pasture until, one day, he wasn't there anymore.

I will never wake up from this nightmare and can only hope that Geronimo spent the rest of his life happily in the care of people who cherished and took good care of him until he died painlessly and peacefully in his sleep—and that he forgave me for my disloyalty.

1980

PART III

CHILDHOOD

CHAPTER 50
BORN TO RIDE!

T he source of my love for horses was puzzling, as I was born in a big city environment not even remotely associated with horses.

All dressed up and ready to ride, thanks to Santa.
All I need is a pony!
circa 1956

CHAPTER 51

A RANGE HORSE

Perhaps part of my horse craziness can be attributed to growing up in the 1950s and 60s, when Westerns abounded on television. I was "glued to the tube" during *Big Valley*, *Cheyenne*, *Bonanza*, *Death Valley Days*, *Gunsmoke*, *The Lone Ranger*, *Maverick*, *The Rifleman*, *Roy Rogers and Dale Evans*, *Wagon Train*, etc. Images on those shows inspired this poem sometime during late childhood or early adolescence.

Beneath the twinkling starlit sky,
Among the swirling clouds of leaves,
A dusty mare gives birth to colt
Near rippling grass and trees.

What a handsome stallion he will be
This funny, bony creature!
With his four long legs
And fine breeding in every feature!

He grew up on the barren plain
And lived through many a season.
It was a carefree, fun-filled life,
But one with a definite reason.

AT HOME ON A HORSE IN THE WOODS

This young colt had a goal to fulfill.
Like most young colts he was foolish —
Defiant, he challenged his leader.
To lead a herd was his determined wish.

A black stallion rose to the challenge.
A scarred old fellow was he;
Deep of shoulder and a fighter at heart,
His wounds screamed of previous victory.

A great commotion arose on the plain.
Two whirling, writhing bodies rushed.
They slashed each other to the bloody finish —
Until the old leader lay hushed.

If you ever visit the barren plain
Look for a herd at dawn.
See the aging leader of the band
Who forever leads his charges on.

undated

PART IV

Last Words

CHAPTER 52
INTERTWINED AND
EMBELLISHED HEART STRINGS

I started Swishtails Custom Horsehair Jewelry in 2013, with the goal of creating keepsakes for clients bonded to their horses. In preparation for Derby 2015, Delanor, my jewelry mentor, commissioned some short braids for her new earring concept. I made several sets of different braids from varied colors and patterns with an assortment of end caps and clasps. When I saw how Delanor incorporated my braids into her design, I wanted a custom pair to commemorate my three "boys."

The earrings had to be of my favorite braid, an 8-string round pattern, difficult to make with horsehair. Years ago, before learning to braid myself, I had seen it on a horsehair braider's website, but neither of my two eventual teachers knew the pattern. Ultimately, I discovered it on YouTube. Long weeks of practice followed—first with parachute cord to learn the fingering, and then applying the fingering to plies of thinner, slicker, and less cooperative horsehair. Selecting the pattern and colors for my earrings was easy—spirals of Dancer's white hair and Highlander's red. The execution, however, was more challenging.

Because mane hair is fine and short, tail hair is usually used for jewelry. I wanted pure red, the color of Highlander's mane and body, for the braid, but his tail hair is a mix of red, black, white, and clear—sometimes in a single strand! I could either harvest and sort through a lot of multi-colored hairs, in search of enough all-red hairs, or cut off just the amount of needed mane hair. As the latter alternative allowed Highlander the opportunity to better continue swishing away parasitic and pain-causing insects, my choice was obvious.

The next challenge was Dancer's hair—white near the rump but yellowed near the ground. Because I'd been taught that it's impossible to wash away the yellow, I was stuck with the uneven coloration. Fortunately, however, half the hairs in a braid are arranged from rump (where they're thicker) to ground (where they're thinner) and half from ground to rump. This results in the braid maintaining the same thickness throughout its entire length. (If all the hairs were arranged in the same direction, the braid would taper like a carrot.)

The result of this hair arrangement, in Dancer's case, would be a continuous cream braid, instead of a white one merging into yellow. Then, because the textures of Highlander's mane hair and Dancer's tail hair differed, I experimented to determine the ratio of red mane hairs to white tail hairs necessary, not only to create equally wide spirals, but also to fit into the end caps.

Once the hairs were selected, balanced, twisted, and plaited, I glued and crimped them into sterling silver end caps. It was then time for Delanor to add the sterling silver ear mounts and end charms she'd designed.

But it didn't seem right that the earrings, made to honor my three favorite horses, were only braided from the hair of two, as I hadn't saved any of Geronimo's hair. At first, because he'd been red and white, I told myself just to pretend that his hairs were incorporated into the braid. But I would always know that they weren't and wanted him to have a distinct presence of his own.

Upon recalling that Geronimo's eyes weren't brown like Dancer's and Highlander's, I asked Delanor to attach a blue bead to each braid. After consulting upon the right shade, Delanor added a pair of blue Swarovski crystals to the design.

I love wearing my earrings. I enjoy looking at them in the mirror and telling people their story. And I love their magic—no matter where I am, I can immediately, with a single magical tug, conjure up precious memories of my three godsends, many recorded in this book—Geronimo, Dancer's Streak, and Highlander.

Post Script: Designing custom horsehair jewelry is not only a creative outlet that helps me to pay Highlander's bills and serve others, it's a blessing—I get to hear wonderful tales from clients about the beloved horses, people, and ponies in their lives.

Earrings designed by Delanor Manson,
Koi Gallery, Louisville, KY.
Photographer: Letha Cupp

2015

CHAPTER 53
AGONY AND ECSTASY

When I returned Highlander to his pasture after our easy, hour-long ride—during which he acted totally normal—he uncharacteristically lay down next to his hay feeder rather than standing and eating from it. Restless, he rolled from one side to another, got up, walked a few feet and lay down again. Sometimes he lay like a lamb, his front feet tucked under him, his back legs folded to one side, and his head up. Other times, he lay full out on one side, his neck and head on the ground and all four legs stretched out.

Concerned, but trying to remain calm, I called and left a message for his longtime vet. The vet called back to say that Highlander was exhibiting the classic signs of colic (abdominal pain) and requested me to text Highlander's pulse and a video of his movements. Doc added that he was headed into surgery and would check his phone and reply as soon as he was able.

I berated myself. I didn't have a stethoscope nor had I ever used one on a horse. I ran to a drug store and purchased one. I could find my own heartbeat with it, but not Highlander's. My cell phone battery was almost dead, and I had never done any videotaping or video-texting.

The stable owner and I began calling other vets and found one willing to make a barn call to a new patient. Then she requested Highlander's temperature!

How stupid and irresponsible could I be? I didn't have a thermometer at the barn and had never taken a horse's temperature.

I had been so lucky—the only time Highlander had ever needed veterinary services was for his annual physical—shots, sheath cleaning, teeth floating, and, when I first got him, for treatment of a mole under one eye. Heck, my 22¾-year-old boy had never even lost a shoe during my 15 years of ownership.

Highlander began improving just before the vet arrived. She was very caring, as one of her horses had died from colic. After taking Highlander's vital signs, she gave him a mild sedative and donned a long plastic glove that covered her flat, diamond-less wedding band and extended all the way to her shoulder. She gently inserted her entire arm into his rectum, checking for an obstruction. Fortunately, all she found was normally formed manure.

Concluding that Highlander was recovering from a mild bout of colic, she opted not to run an endoscope, or a tube, up his nose and down to his stomach. Rather, she gave him a shot of Banamine to ease his pain. He was stalled for the night and only fed a half a flake of hay after his sedative wore off and a whole flake two hours later. The vet left a tube of Banamine paste just in case it might be necessary the next day. (It wasn't.)

The day after that, I headed to the barn for some dedicated practice with my newly-purchased stethoscope and thermometer. Both Highlander's temp and pulse were normal, so we headed out for a short ride. The weather was nippy, and it was an hour before dark, so I chose my favorite hour loop—a mostly curved one-track through the woods that began and ended at two different points of a gravel road. The trail, obscured by crunchy leaves, was fun to track. I pretended I was a Native American. As the woods darkened, Highlander and I began trotting the curves and cantering the straight-aways in a race to catch the light still lingering on the open, gravel road.

I absolutely love riding at dusk and when Highlander is super-energized. My stress melted away, my youth returned, and I had a blast. I was so very grateful to have my boy back again. The—very happy, thanks be to God—End.

December, 2016

Appendix I
Trail Riding Safety Tips

Trail Riding Safety Tips: Risk accompanies the joy of trail riding. So before heading onto the trails, heed this advice: "Always be prepared" and "An ounce of prevention is worth a pound of cure." These maxims from the Boy Scouts and Ben Franklin apply to riders young and old because our goal is the same—to ride safely for as long as we wish and are physically able. While we can't eliminate all accidents, we can reduce their occurrence and severity by giving prevention serious forethought.

1. Ride with someone if you can. When you ride alone, leave a note stating the time you're leaving the barn, the route you're taking, your expected time of return, your cell phone number, and the number of an emergency contact. When you ride with someone, make sure you know their emergency contact information.

2. Carry these items on your person (in a bag or fanny pack)—they won't do you any good if you fall off your horse and it runs away with them.

   - Bandana: It can serve as a towel, dressing, pressure bandage, sling, handkerchief, or scarf. Tied around your nose bandit style, it can filter out dust kicked up by the horses in front of you. It can even serve as an emergency toilet wipe. To keep your bandana clean before use or confined afterward, carry it in a small plastic bag.

- Bridle pass: (if required on the public land you ride on)

- Canvas bag: for carrying the litter you pick up (thank you!), especially the glass bottles. (I know of a horse that bled to death after stepping on a shard.)

- Cell phone: (perhaps with a GPS app)

- First aid kit for yourself and vet wrap for your horse

- Flashlight

- Hoof pick

- Identifications: (e.g., a runner's ID bracelet)

- Insect repellent: (for you and your horse)

- Medical information: (perhaps a photocopy of your medical insurance card)

- Sharp tool: (e.g., knife, scissors, clippers, etc.) for emergency tack repairs and vegetation pruning

- Snack

- Sunscreen

- Tack-repair materials: (twine, shoe laces, leather cords, zip ties, duct tape, etc.)

- Toilet paper: Carry it in a clean plastic bag, and bring along an extra bag for carrying soiled paper home. (Please do not toss soiled TP on or next to the trail. Yes, it will eventually biodegrade, but no one wants to observe the process.)

- Trail map

- Water bottle: (for keeping hydrated; washing your hands, face, or a wound; rewetting the bandana you tied around your neck in the heat, etc.)

- Whistle: (in case you get lost or need to scare off some wildlife)

3. Wear a helmet when you ride. Even a well-trained horse will shy at a dashing deer or flee from a swarm of disturbed yellow jackets.

4. Dress appropriately. Wear boots with heels to prevent your feet from slipping through your stirrups; protect yourself from thorns, bugs, spider webs, and sunburn by wearing long pants and sleeved shirts; add a detachable sun visor to your helmet; tie a plastic poncho to the back of your saddle or stuff a slicker into your saddle bag when rain is forecast (most rain coats will not protect your saddle); don an orange sweatshirt or jacket during hunting season; wear a fluorescent vest with reflective stripes on trafficked roads; dress in layers, etc.

5. Put identification on your horse to increase the odds of its recovery should it run off without you. Consider micro-chipping or branding (iron or freeze), or attach ID tags to your horse's halter and bridle. (Dog and luggage tags work well.)

6. Adorn your horse appropriately. During fly season, use a mesh riding mask and a mesh rump rug. During hunting season, attach bells to your saddle and orange fleece wraps around the bridle straps and breast band. During cold winters, tie a fleece rump rug to the back of your saddle.

7. Practice good trail etiquette: maintain a safe distance from the horse in front of you; tie a red ribbon to your horse's tail if it's prone to kicking; communicate when passing other riders; only canter and gallop on straightaways to

prevent collisions with oncoming horses; don't muddy the entire stream when stopping to water your horse; etc.

8. Always, always, be aware of your horse and alert to everything around you. Keep in mind that horses are highly sensitive prey animals prone to flight when spooked.

9. Do not overtax your horse. Put in the time necessary to slowly condition it to go the distance and at the pace you want as well as to navigate the required ascents and descents on the trails you take.

10. Work other forms of exercise into your daily routine to keep yourself in shape for riding. As you age, consider Pilates or yoga classes for whole-body workouts to stretch your muscles, challenge your flexibility and balance, and maintain your core strength. Your horse will benefit because our bodies play off of each other. Consider scheduling massages and chiropractic adjustments, not only for yourself, but also for your steed.

11. Consider taking out insurance that will financially protect you, your horse, others, and any property involved in a horse-related accident.

Remember the adage you heard when you first started riding—"It's not *if* you'll fall off, it's *when?*" Likewise, "It's not *if* you'll have an accident on the trail, it's *what kind and how serious?*" To decrease your odds of trouble and to increase your relaxation and enjoyment, prepare carefully and ride defensively.

Happy trails!

Appendix II
Self-Study/Discussion Questions

Considering some of the following questions may provide you with helpful clarity as you pursue your dream. You can journal your answers privately or discuss them with others, perhaps during a book club meeting.

1. Which of your life's dreams have you already achieved?

2. Which unmanifested dream is most important to you right now?

3. Do you know when, where, and/or how this dream arose? (It might stem from your childhood or be on your bucket list.)

4. Have you taken any steps toward achieving this dream? Which ones?

5. Do you know what your next step is, or do you currently feel stuck, overwhelmed, and/or ready to give up on your dream?

6. If you do not know your next step, have you asked anyone for help? If so, who agreed and how did they help you?

7. What have you learned from the steps that you tried that didn't work out?

8. Do you believe that your dream is legitimate and that you are worthy of attaining it?

9. Have you ever considered that your dream might have been planted in you by the Creator?

10. Are you willing to take just one step forward in pursuit of your dream without knowing all the steps beyond it? Are you open to considering that the necessary steps will be revealed when the time is right? (Saying and meaning "yes" should free you to move forward and build momentum.)

11. Do you accept that no one, including you, can attain your dream independently (without help)?

12. We live in a noisy world, filled with so many voices—those of our family, our co-workers, our Facebook friends, the news, etc. How do you, or might you, disconnect for a while and concentrate on hearing your own thoughts and God's guidance?

13. How do you determine which steps God, not your ego or other people, is guiding you to take?

14. Which steps can you execute on your own, and which do you need help with? Besides God, who else can you ask for support and to rejoice in your successes?

My childhood dream for permanent connection to horses came true during middle age when a minister unexpectedly told me that God had planted it in me upon my creation and that God would not stop knocking on my heart until I fully accepted it. That was the missing key for me—as soon as I accepted that, my dream came true quickly, in ways I'd never imagined. Twenty years later, it's still unfolding. This book is part of the process.

Best of luck in distinguishing your dream, accepting it as your divine calling, and taking the action steps necessary for its attainment. You will improve your life in ways you can't imagine right now, become more of the person God created you to be, and contribute your special gift to the world.

Appendix III
READER REVIEWS

Inspiring... made me want to give my horses a hug and thank them for letting me ride them through the woods and trails with a new appreciation for the beauty and wonder of nature. Dreams can come true. *Gretchen M.*

As a lifetime horse owner, I have to say that I LOVE this book! I'm taking my time reading it. I'm tempted to devour it, but instead I will savor it the same way I consume my last piece of dark chocolate. *Susan V.*

A series of beautifully written essays and prose poems that come together as a memoir/meditation by one woman's love and transcendent connection to all things equine. [The Author] opens her life and heart to the reader, sharing her personal struggles, longings, joys, and spiritual journey as well as her ever-widening discovery along the way of the beauty and wonder of God's world through the beloved horses in her life. *Patti L.*

A beautiful and relaxing ride through the lovely woods, on the back of a trusted best friend. The author is both a scientist and a very spiritual person and shows us what can be experienced when the two traits combine. This book is a beautiful tribute to the relationship between humans and horses and to being aware of, and frequently in awe of, your surroundings in nature. The author experiences the joys of living in the present and shares her joy with her beautiful words and an open heart. I will definitely read it again, and I will love it again. *Bev A.*

Ride with Jan as she explores the many facets that life with horses and time alone on the trail can bring. Her memoir is filled with imagery as she brings out the unique surroundings of her favorite spots to explore. As seasons change so do the trails change, not only in color but in footing as well. Each chapter promises a new adventure, whether it is getting "lost" or finding that your path is being shared with other forest dwellers...[Alexander's] knowledge and philosophical insights flow throughout the book. You will also meet up with the three horses that have held such a special place in her life. This is a book that can be read and re-read. Enjoy the ride! *Mary B.*

Janet Alexander has written a beautiful book! This gem is a meditative and relaxing ride down the bridle trail, exploring the natural world around us as well as the world within. Highly recommended! *Karen F.*

This book is inspiring, heartfelt, and joyous. Taking my time in each chapter, I'm lifted to the moments described. This is a book you feel your way through. I was brought to tears many times upon reading the metaphoric conclusions and "God aspect" the author reveals. *Kathy S.*

Started reading [this] book yesterday. It's wonderful. I love the pictures it paints for me. Not just visual pics but the feelings it makes me feel too. I've only read to chapter 11. But it's a book that also wants me to stop reading so I can savor the images before moving on. *Vicki M.*

Janet is an astute observer who captured vivid and revealing details of her heart, her horse, and their shared environment. By writing down her observations and feelings immediately after their birth, they remain forever fresh. Her gifted writing put us right in the woods with her and Highlander. We could almost feel it, smell it, and step in it! The influence of the Spirit on Janet's soul, life, and writing is apparent in this excerpt from her memoir: "In close physical contact and companionable silence, he (Highlander) and I enjoy life and appreciate the beauty of God's creation together. Riding is a form of prayer." Amen and thanks to Janet for sharing the happy trails. *Larry G.*

ABOUT THE AUTHOR

Kathy Schaeffer

Janet is a retired science teacher who loves nature and lives in Southern Indiana with her husband, Jim, and their cats and dogs. She boards her horse Highlander at a stable adjacent to state property with extensive riding trails. (God's sense of humor tickles her—the stable's name is The Circle C and this book has a © symbol.)

Besides writing, Janet also braids horsehair jewelry to help horse lovers celebrate the special bonds they've developed with their equines.

Comments regarding Janet's book or jewelry can be sent to swishtails.com. She loves hearing from her readers about their ultimate dreams.

Made in the USA
Columbia, SC
09 June 2022

61554876R00089